RELIGION WITHOUT MAGIC

PHILLIPS ENDECOTT OSGOOD, minister of the First Unitarian Church of Essex County, Orange, New Jersey, is president of the Liberal Ministers Association of Greater New York. He was formerly president of the House of Clerical and Lay Deputies (General Convention of the Episcopal Church). Among Dr. Osgood's previously published books are *Solomon's Temple, Church Year Sermons for Children, Pulpit Dramas, Old-Time Church Drama Adapted,* and *Say I to Myself.*

Religion Without Magic

Phillips Endecott Osgood

THE BEACON PRESS · BOSTON

Library of Congress Catalog Card Number: 54-8427

Printed in U.S.A.

TO EUNICE,
MY COMPLETE COMRADE,
MY WIFE;
WITHOUT WHOM THIS BOOK
COULD NEVER HAVE BEEN WRITTEN

Contents

Author's Note ix

BOOK ONE
RELIGION WITH MAGIC

1. Infiltration by Magic 3
2. The Sin of Ecclesiastical Professionalism . . 15
3. Roman Catholicism 26
4. The Problems of Judaism 40
5. The Sin of Sectarianism 48
6. Christian Science 68
7. Credulities 73
8. Christianity and Non-Christian Faiths . . . 92

An Interpolated Note 106

BOOK TWO
RELIGION WITHOUT MAGIC

9. Half-Liberals and Honest Doubt 111
10. Is the Bible Outmoded? 127
11. The Son of Man 139
12. Prayer? Worship? Sacraments? 151
13. What Has Science To Say? 171
14. Is Immortality Logical? 180
15. Comrades of the Carpenter! 193

Author's Note

Lincoln's words "with malice toward none and charity for all" far too frequently are quoted without the succeeding phrase, "with firmness in the right as God gives us to see the right." That first phrase, without the balancing one, can be interpreted as a merely sentimental amiability. It needs the sterner ideal of firmness in the right as God gives us to see the right. Both malice-free charity and firmness in convictions are commanded by human decency.

Particularly in its first half, this book will be called intolerant by those whose prejudices and conventional religious ideas are analyzed here. It will be branded as uncharitable and malicious by pietists of the traditional pattern.

But let it be said at the outset that this volume is written in the desperate hope that its mood will be understood. If religion is to be the democratic concern it should be, there must be liberty for judgments between earnest servants of its deepest cause. There is no place for dictatorship in it.

Jesus said, "Judge not, that ye be not judged." He can't have meant that there should be no evaluations or judgments between men. He himself proved in all he said and did that he was not proposing an innocuous Milquetoast inanity. Didn't he mean, "Don't judge others unless you are willing to be judged yourself"? By the standard you measure, you must open-mindedly accept measurement. He recommended adult good sportsmanship, in a fair field with no favors. Give-and-take frankness in mutual good will should allow even major surgery of cancerous opinions, for the very reason that the human being who holds them is too important as a person among persons to go unchallenged. But to lose the spirit of charity and slide over into malice is dictatorship or bigotry. To be without firmness in the right as God—or our dispassionate logic—gives us to see the right is to reduce mutual relations to fatuousness.

If I am wrong or if my rightness is only partial, I should welcome the opponent who cares enough to present to me his proof, not his demands for my surrender to his assumed infallibility. I do not want to be "tolerated." (Emerson said the word is an insult.) I want his acid-tested facts, as he sees them, placed beside my own—all in a common enthusiasm for the truth for its own sake. Freedom is for those who are really able to *think* for themselves—*forward*. It is not for those who are so weak that they yearn for authority's directives to save them from the responsibility of self-direction. The power complex violates the sixth commandment against murder; for if character is the sum total of decisions one makes for himself, a ready-made dictum kills it in proportion to the puppetry it compels.

Even if these chapters hurt over-sensitive conformists, the author has spoken only for the cause of religious realism as he sees it. Isn't there justification for hatred of harmful influences along with a caring for the worths of those people who are conditioned by them? As William Watson writes:

> No spendthrifts of our hate are we.
> Our hate is used with husbandry.
> We hold our hate too choice a thing
> For light and careless lavishing.
> We cannot, dare not make it cheap!
> For holy uses will we keep
> A thing so pure, a thing so great
> As Heaven's benignant gift of hate.
> Is there no ancient, sceptered Wrong?
> No numbing power, endured too long?

Yea! And for those our hatred shall
Be cloistered and kept virginal!

With utter willingness to be shown where he is factually
and provably wrong, and with a deep realization of everyman's authentic birthright, the author casts this book into the
arena, even to the lions. If it is remembered that a sincere
and a sympathetic charity may go with strong conviction,
may it be hoped that such an appraisal as this will find some
open-minded readers who will judicially weigh its presenta-
tion.

P.E.O.

BOOK ONE

RELIGION WITH MAGIC

CHAPTER ONE

Infiltration by Magic

The next chapter of the reformation of Christianity is over-due. The Protestant Reformation was only the first stage in the needed re-forming of Christianity.

Moderns deserve a factually based religion which can command both their self-respect and their common sense. They must be freed from sentimentalism, and unscientific credulity, and the dogmas of all outmoded, professionalized authoritarianisms. Twentieth-century adults demand a religion in absolute accord with axioms of scientific thinking. They want the laboratory method for faith.

Such a religion is tragically lacking in the traditional churches, where it is smothered by institutionalized unrealism — an artificial and fantastic theology based on the pretense of magic. The simplicity, humanness, and spontaneous intuitions of Jesus of Nazareth have been overlaid and traduced until the truths he taught and lived are well-nigh hidden by the ecclesiasticism which claims his sponsorship.

The Protestant Reformation merely scratched the surface of the Christian essentials. To be sure, it clarified the issue of man's inherent right to spontaneous sincerities insofar as the Roman Church had strait-jacketed them. But it substituted another authoritarianism, that of the "inspired" Bible, competitively interpreted by rival communions which built their unstable structures on their founders' fiats. The Reformation declared a few great principles of faith, but the further implications of these were unguessed by the reformers.

Thereafter the denominations more or less settled on the lees of their special achievement, but were satisfied thenceforth to "read the minutes of the last meetings" for self-congratulations as non-Romans. In the assumption that the Reformation was sufficient, Protestants have been prone to define their credo too acrimoniously in its anti-Catholic terms. They have forgotten that the first syllable of the Protestant name is not *anti* but *pro,* and the very pronunciation of the inclusive title has ceased to be *Pro*testantism. The idea of *pro*test has for them become negative.

This book presumes to raise the issue of a progressive *Pro*testantism which will strike at all perversions of realistic religion—that is, *it will strike at the root of the whole ideology of magic.* This contention is no farfetched fanaticism, nor is it a merely academic issue. *No matter how uncomfortable it may be for traditionalists to face it, the fact undeniably is that the assumption of magic has so honeycombed all the recognized orthodox faiths that the danger of losing essential religion is catastrophic.*

Magic? Let's understand what the word means before we follow its vestigial ramifications in the churches.

Webster's Dictionary defines magic as "The art, or body of arts, which claims or is believed to be able to compel a deity or supernatural power to do or to refrain from doing some act or to change temporarily the order of natural events, or which claims or is believed to produce effects by the assistance of supernatural beings, as angels, demons, or departed spirits, or by a mastery of secret forces in nature."

Notice that the compilers of this definition refrained from the inclusion of God by saying "*a* deity" and "supernatural beings," but there is no logic in the omission. A magic which claims to compel the Almighty is the greatest impudence and presumption. The amplification of the above definition is additionally pertinent: "magic is not clearly differentiated from science by primitive peoples. It is a part of most primitive religions." Even so. Then the survival of primitive ideas in our modern, scientific day is an even worse superstition. This survival was possible because "on white or natural magic no ban was placed." Nor has it yet been placed.

Lest one dictionary should be accused of bias, other and parallel definitions can be marshaled. The *Oxford Dictionary* says magic is "the pretended art of influencing the course of events and producing marvelous physical phenomena." The *Britannica* says: "The word magic is still used, as in the ancient world, to include a confused mass of beliefs and practices, hardly agreeing except in being beyond those ordinary actions of cause and effect which men accustomed to their regularity have come to regard as merely natural. . . . The great characteristic of magic is its unreality." Hasting's *Encyclopedia of Religion and Ethics* flatly calls magic "a general name for all the bad kinds of trafficking with the occult powers and supra-sensible in vogue in a given society." This is written by no less a scholar than R. R. Marrett, who also bluntly epitomizes: "As the folklorist knows, a permanent possibility of demoralizing superstition lurks in human nature and only education in regard to both physical and moral truths can keep the monster down." What is there in all this which forbids the hypothetical application of this estimate to contemporary religion as institutionalism presents it? Can the churches prove themselves guiltless of the listed varieties of "sympathetic magic, divination, thaumaturgy, and incantation"? However "white" their occultism may be, isn't it colored by magic, "that bastard sister of science"?

Because the institution cannot easily change itself, it is understandable that traditional churches attract members who would be uncomfortable with change. The atmosphere of melodramatic "medicine" makes them believe that transactions with the mysteriously shrouded Godhead are being accomplished on their behalf. Few of them know their way in the maze of complicated casuistry, although the officials are so familiar with it that they have come to believe in their own sorcery. The chanted phrases of blood sacrifice, the "paschal lamb slain from the foundation of the world," the "saving cross," of sacramental "grace" to the faithful, of inspiration, of "Christ's eternal high priesthood before the God whom he also is," of Trinitarian interrelation in One Being—these are the High Abracadabra which suffice.

Among primeval folk magic and science were indistinguishable from each other in their embryonic stages. We can have sympathy for those first children of nature in their fumbling attempts to find means to safety, victory, health, love, birth, and immortality amidst the awesome mysteries of the unexplained universe. They glimpsed natural law, but the mystery still overwhelmed their knowledge, and their magic eclipsed their science. But that era is over—or should be. It is to be feared that the 1884 *Britannica* is right when it ruefully says, "Looked at as a series of delusions, magic is distasteful to the modern mind, which *when once satisfied of its practical futility,* is apt to discard it as folly unworthy of further notice. . . . The universal diffusion of magical ideas among mankind, *excepting only the limited class who have abandoned them through higher education,* shows that we are here in the presence of a deep-seated intellectual process."[1]

The whole discussion in the chapters that follow here

---

[1]Vol. XV, p. 205; italics mine.

is precisely on this specific issue: *can religion divest itself of magic pretense?* It is an issue so fundamental and involves ideas and customs which so permeate traditional religion that many or perhaps most adherents will refuse to recognize that it exists. For the obedient majority of the faithful, religion is as the churches have purveyed it in magic formulae, doctrine, and ritual.

Gilbert Chesterton used to say that in any debate the first necessity is to sharpen the terms of it to an exact point— therefore the foregoing definition and preliminary critique of magic. But also there are three terms for which no synonyms have the same overtones; these terms must be used over and over in such a discussion as this. They are *realism, radicalism,* and *liberalism.* We'd best sharpen them to the point of meaning they have, at least in this survey of contemporary religion.

Realism? The word usually carries an emotional implication which is cynical, as though to the realist all ideals were hallucinations. This is unfair. For, rightly understood, realism does not connote a debunking of the spiritualities or a hard-boiled scorn of sound sentiment and sane mysticism. It should mean the recognition of *all* the reality which can be demonstrated or deduced either in the material world or in psychological, historical, and spiritual experience. It extends the scientific habit of mind beyond external data and follows it into psychology and intellect, philosophy and faith. It does not limit validity to the narrow body of mastered laboratory findings; rather is its logic reverently impelled beyond them by the clue of reason until they are seen to point to the nature of the universals—as a fragment of crystal is as crystalline as the total crystal. Realism includes the ideal, of which we know the indices, as Plato explained the idea of the ultimate oak tree operative in the acorn. So "realism" is not ruthless disenchantment except when it reveals *un*realism. Religion and realism should be one. Religion without magic is high realism.

The term *radicalism,* in this day of its glib use as a derogatory label, has also been doctored by an unfair bias and has gathered an opprobrium beyond its deserts. Granted that there is an incidental axiom in it of rebellion against reactionary stuffiness; nevertheless, the indignation of orthodox pietists who have avoided that pain in the mind which is the start of high realism, who are shocked when the revolutionaries pull off long-worn velvet gloves to handle the sacrosanctities with bare hands—this indignation is not the main emphasis of the word. Look at its derivation: it comes from *radix,* a root. Hence it suggests digging down to the root of things. Arithmetic uses its radicals and a surgeon speaks of a radical operation. A right radicalism in religion delves down to the basic fundamentals which no fundamentalist dares stress: a true religion underneath all religions. This truly radical religion is that of our deepest human instincts, the outreach of our human spontaneities, the subsoil richness of all unspoiled character in its goodness and strength, the intuitive experience of the life in which, however we mishandle it, we live and move and have our being. It is perhaps unconsciously apprehended and it is certainly unphrasable with any adequacy, but it is the universal birthright of significance from that creative source of all worth which for lack of a more untrammeled name we may still call God.

Liberalism? Repetitiously but earnestly we say it too is a popularly misconceived label. For liberalism is not, as many believe, a blurred vagueness of self-satisfied conviction, a drifting faith which has lost its moorings. Liberalism is not libertarianism. It is not only freedom *from* but freedom *for* and *forward*. Dr. Burdette Backus cannily discriminates that liberalism is not what is prevalently called "free thought," for liberalism's freedom is "freedom to discipline your mind for the discovery of truth. You are free to examine the evidence and to accept the conclusions which you believe to be required by that evidence. Paradoxically, you are free to believe, not what you *want* to, but what you *have* to believe as a consequence of having disciplined your intelligence to follow those methods which experience demonstrates as most effective to arrive at the truth. The term 'free thinker' is more accurately used of the orthodox who believe, let us say, that Balaam's ass talked. They are free to believe the impossible; we (liberals) are not." [2]

As Huxley answered his defamers in the Victorian day of agnosticism's ordeal, "Orthodoxy is the Bourbon of the world of thought: it learns not, neither can it forget."

The liberal's own realization of the greatness of truth makes him humble, not scornful. He cannot march in goose-stepping conformity to shibboleths: spiritual fascism is unthinkable for him. Liberal religion presupposes a democracy of self-determined values and constructive integrities.

Now, what of the status of Western religion? There is the reactionary membership inside the traditional churches; there are the half-liberals still nominally of church membership; there is the vast company of secessionists, among whom are all the groups of Humanists, Ethical Culturists, agnostics and so-called atheists. In one way or another, in all these groups, the moot thesis for defense or attack is that of *magic*.

---

[2]"May Week Sermon," in *The Christian Register*, August 1951, pp. 14-17.

Official churchdom is hypnotized into the acceptance of the magic as the validation of its dogma and ritual. If objectivity were possible for fundamentalists, they could not but perceive the characteristics of ecclesiastical necromancy. The ancient shaman or medicine man, wearing his demon mask with its vulture's feathers, whirling his bull-roarer and boasting of his accompanying but invisible leopards whose lashing tails must be shunned on pain of death, is not unimaginably the confrere of the vested, pontificating priest at his Mass who asserts (as a leading Anglo-Catholic once blandly asserted) that when the Sanctus bell sounds at the words of the consecration of the bread and wine, he "holds the whole God in (his) hands" and administers "the whole God" to the communicants.[3]

The Roman Catholic Church is quintessentially magic: that is its cornerstone thesis. Nor is Protestantism exempt. Sectarianism is based on competitive infallibilities of bibliolatry. The doctrine of the Scriptures' inspiration to the amanuenses of the Holy Spirit brings its oracular *verbatim et literatim* authority to the pitch of something more than miracle. From their varying deductions the denominations build their concepts of the valid form of baptism, closed communion, "election," and so on. Whether they are Roman, Anglo-Catholic, fundamentalist, average Protestant, or fringe cultist, they are all shareholders of a common body of doctrine with differing interpretations only in the minor confessional or administrational ways. They all accept the cardinal doctrines of a pre-existing, virgin-born, miraculous, and miracle-working Christ, whose earthly parenthesis between

---

[3]This doctrine comfortingly reassures the recipients, however, that "God magically removes the flesh and blood of the Crucified from the elements before digestion begins"!

incarnation and ascension was a magic interlude in his transcendent and eternal glory "at the right hand of the Father." In him, they allege, was "the fullness of the Godhead bodily." His words and works were a superhuman revelation; his crucifixion, foreordained from timeless time, was the sacrifice which the Father needed to enable him to give his "grace of salvation" to the sinful children of Adam. The Church is now assumed to be the body of Christ on earth, endowed with his powers, to prepare for the Last Assize and eternal reward or damnation of quick and dead!

The Church's thesis of revelation, a supernatural Savior, and an errorless church cannot stand up under test. And there are many, many moderns who cannot swallow this thesis. They discount its literal truth, taking the manifestos of the past with many grains of salt. Such mental reservationists are obnoxious to the strictly orthodox, but the pressure of modernism is too strong for the hierarchies openly to ban them. Therefore, except in the Catholic and fundamentalist camps, there is a reluctant permission for these semi-heretics to continue inside the fold by the expedient of "symbolic interpretation." They are tacitly permitted to say the creeds in a Pickwickian sense, tongue in cheek. They are tolerated as Exhibit A of the inclusiveness and broad-mindedness of the fellowship. Only it is hoped that they will not be too vocal with their dissents on the virgin birth, miracles, and the physical resurrection because, after all, the doctrines of the incarnation and the atonement are the rock bottom ones which are supposed to be kept untouched by such surface doubts. In this assumed immunity from question, the dogmas down underneath remain hypothetically safe—whatever the uneasiness that someday the liberals will discover that they have exercised themselves only over the secondary questions of "how" instead of "what." If these semi-heretics ever waken to their mistake and begin a philosophic attack on the citadel doctrines, authority will be in a more serious dilemma. Gingerly modification by sugar-coating phrases here and there would not then avail to save the threatened doctrines.

As a typical example of carrying water on both shoulders in the present stage of disaffection over nonbasic incidentals, here is a true anecdote. A disturbed bishop insisted that one of his leading churches, which had been served by a too liberal minister, should amend its constitution by adding: "This Parish accedes to the Canons, Doctrines, Discipline and Worship of the . . . church and acknowledges its authority." But one important and indignant parishioner announced that he neither would nor could renounce his inalienable right to do his own religious thinking; whereat his new minister wrote in reply, "I assure you that this is a legal technicality that binds you to no practices or beliefs. I can readily concur in many of your points of view about doctrine. I am not in the least interested in theology or Creed. . . . Not to pass this amendment would stir up the legal beagles; to pass it will make no difference in what we do or believe here."

Evangelical tolerance differs from fundamentalist anathematizing of liberals, whether the fundamentalism be the pre-Reformation Catholicism (Roman or Greek or Anglican) or the Reformation kind. However gentle, sunny, and humane evangelicalism may be, its urbanity is not as nominated in the bond of original convenants or creeds. The tolerance of easygoing comradeship has the virtue of charity for which one's heart warms; but the fact remains that orthodoxy *as such* forbids that virtue in relation to its definitive tenets. If the implicit defenders of "the faith once for all delivered" ever got the whip hand and were moved to push their strict criteria, where would the mental reservationists be? Increasingly, this is not beyond imagining; for the guardians of orthodoxy are gathering strength in this era when the maelstrom of insecurity terrifies those who fly for refuge to authority.

The mental reservationists are in an anomalous position. They try to hold the holy oil of orthodoxy and the water of realism in an emulsion which cannot be a true blend. They take to themselves the permission, like Naaman's, to worship in a house of Rimmon, in the dogma of which they do not believe but which is the established church of their society—meanwhile inwardly holding to a truth they have learned over the border in the alien country of scientific factuality. It is to them in particular that this book is addressed, although it also is focused on those radicals who do not know how really religious they are.

What a pity it is that self-styled atheists have come to their violence of secession from institutional tradition without recognizing that their recoil has only cleared the ground for their free exercise of constructive faith. Over and over again realists grow sick at heart to hear rebels fulminate against the Christianity which its devotees represent as the only saving revelation, those rebels being apparently unaware that there is a third alternative between magicized churchianity and the sweeping condemnation of *all* religion. This third alternative is the secessionists' instinctive humanism, which could be developed into a legitimate faith by sane, reverently agnostic deduction.

It is an uncomfortable historic fact that the heretics, not the conformists, have been the ones who advanced the cause of truth. The list is too long to catalog, but it includes Akhnaton, the prophets, Lao-tze, Jesus of Nazareth, Socrates, Plato,

Aeschylus, Euripides, Galileo, Socinus, Servetus, Spinoza, Priestley, Paine, Jefferson, Ingersoll, Huxley, Emerson, Parker, Gandhi, Schweitzer, and Einstein. These and their comrades are the deeply conscientious, courageous self-contributors, nobly faithful to the human essentials. The copybook cliché that "there is more faith in honest doubt than there is in half the creeds" has been written into the story of civilization in letters of flame and blood by rebels and martyrs.

Until the idea of magic is at last deleted from official Christianity, the Church's place in the modern world will be increasingly challenged. If magic *were* real, it would violate the integrity of the universe, baffle honest research, and reduce thinking to dazed bewilderment. The ideology of magic is diametrically against truth; therefore it is *immoral*.

If religion is to inspire adult men and women by providing a rationale of existence, a purpose for living, a worth for personality, a will and a power of ultimate fulfillment, it must be absolutely in affinity with universals and have the backing of demonstrable experience. Magic frustrates all this. It meets the hunger for reality and meaning with specious substitutes. We need religion to live—we need it desperately! *But we need it without magic.*

This book is, first, a modest but resolute documentation of the magic which has perverted the traditional churches; but it is, second, a plea for the religion which the elimination of magic would free for its rightful power. The first chapters are an endeavor to diagnose our present unfortunate state; the second section aims to be constructive, to show the characteristics of the spiritual adventure of which we are capable. Religion *without* magic would be rewarded by its fruits of spontaneity, liberty, conviction, and practical relevance to contemporary problems. Can such a religion be potent until there is a new, further *protestant* reformation?

CHAPTER TWO

The Sin of Ecclesiastical Professionalism

The Martin Luther of the new reformation probably will not be a professional ecclesiast. Perhaps the new reformation will be keynoted not by an individual at all, but by average, earnest laymen.

The professional naturally builds a system. Ecclesiasticism, Jewish and Christian—(also Buddhist, Confucianist, Shintoist, or any other organized faith), demonstrates this. The Christian ecclesiastics may have been unaware of the gradual change by which the spontaneous religion of the wayside Carpenter grew into an institution which comes tragically near to the very ecclesiasticism that brought the Crucifixion to pass. But that is the end result.

Professionals are susceptible to insidious temptations of power. Their specialization in the routine of official mechanics and pronouncements exerts a subtle influence on their belief in their system and therefore in themselves as its manipulators. Since they are so occupied with their academic theories, with their dogmatic dialectics, with the practicalities of regulation and administration, it is small wonder they cannot often get an objective look at themselves. Step by step they advance into a superiority complex, taking it as unquestionable that their office makes them of different clay from the laity. They become convinced that it is their function to do the thinking for their followers and to guide them through the wilderness of life, by expert decisions, into tame dependence. Consequently they themselves tend not to examine long-accepted presuppositions or to examine themselves as to their right to act as oracular representatives of the infallible establishment. They are betrayed into fixities and finalities: they are immunized against searching dissatisfactions. Although the precedents they quote may be of comparatively recent formulation, they ascribe to earlier eras their later ideas, asserting that their present standards are "the faith once for all delivered" to the saints, *semper, ubique et ab omnibus.*

This is the case of the complete professional. In variant degrees partial professionals may have had their qualms about the impeccability of the system, but in the main they have continued in harness. The least hypnotized ones may struggle weakly, pathetically or perhaps heroically. Individually and confidentially among intimates they hesitantly debate whether the literal doctrine and discipline can stand up under scientific examination. They try to freshen the much-breathed air of ancient dogma by opening the windows of "interpretation." But they rationalize their sincerity about saying the creeds. ("Although," says a typical modernist, "it would be much better to have the creeds sung, since that would attract no attention to the meaning of the words, any more than any church anthem does.") The ideal of honesty is sublimated by allegorizing moot articles, or by maintaining that allegiance to the deeper truths allows them to be patronizing about their "quaint phrasing." Naturally, if these disturbed semi-professionals speak out while still bearing the name of officials, they are accused of being mavericks or heretics. If Bishop Barnes of Birmingham, England, had not been protected in his office by governmental appointment, he doubtless would have incurred more than the barrage of merely wrathful invectives from vested authority in the Church against his forthright recent books. As it is, he is branded a traitor and is definitely *persona non grata*. In proportion as such honest people show their fermenting discomfort under the demands of professionalism, they manifest the percentage of honesty still left in them.

While he was asleep, Gulliver was bound down by Lilliputians with thousands of threads; although a giant, he could not free himself. So the inherently vital Christian faith succumbed and was bound fast with thread after thread of imperialist non-Christian notions, until it was prisoner to them.

It is pertinent for us to review the subtle ways in which today's professional institutions became what they are. For they still officially perpetuate their past, in policy and in indoctrination. Even though there may be surface modifications to give the appearance of obedience to pressure for change, these are akin to the tree's bending before a gale but holding fast with its deep roots. The system of doctrine and discipline is saturated with magic and its history must be carefully diagnosed to find how far back we now must cut to rediscover the stark religion of Jesus and the prophets.

Here follows a sketchy retrospect which perhaps can provide a clue to the evolutionary change:

(1) Saul of Tarsus was trained as a Pharisee. He never knew Jesus or heard him preach. Therefore Paul's indirect knowledge had the chance to be colored by his own inherent habit of mind. He saw Jesus through the lenses of Pharisaic dogma and he naturally cast him in the role of the expected Messiah. He transformed the cross into a magic whereby God freed elect human beings from original sin and made men eligible for salvation. He said, "As in Adam all die,

even so in Christ shall all be made alive." Justification was by the acceptance of this in faith!

Paul was a Jew from Asia Minor; therefore he was also half Greek in his thinking. He was steeped in the rationale of the Mystery cults of that world, those ancient freemasonries which took the myths of the savior gods as more than allegorical. The acted-out story of the god who went down into the jaws of death to rescue a beloved one put the participants inside that god's life, and thus inside his conquest of evil and death and into his "anastasis" or victorious resurrection. A god-embodying priest-king became the liaison bearer of sin and giver of life, and the imparter of the divine potence to those baptized in his blood. They ate and drank the sacramental elements in which the mana of the god was present and so they revived their own mana—"having already passed from death into life."

Taken as only philosophically symbolic, the Mysteries could have been magnificently invigorating, but their average membership reduced the pattern to a ritual of guaranteed magic. Paul may have been mystically allegorical in his turgid figures of speech but the Church understood them so literally that under this missionary's dynamic influence, Jesus the prophet and martyr became a Mystery savior god, an atoning and life-giving Messiah such as the Son of Man never claimed to be. For, according to those direct records which fearless sifting of the Gospels gives us, Jesus apparently had no such concepts about himself as Paul's headstrong theologizing according to the contemporary hunger for magic ascribed to him. The Nazarene had his own simple, searching, superbly original, nobly spiritual religion, which is even yet a distinguishable subsurface stream in official Church tradition. But major saint, key person of history, magnificent hero of faith that Paul was, as the "Second Founder of Christianity" he nevertheless deflected the religion Jesus had into a religion of his own foliation, using Jesus as his lay figure.

(2) When Christianity was released from the catacombs and, almost by the toss of a coin, presented with the authority of the established religion of Constantine's empire, we should not be surprised to see that it clutched at imperial organizational power. It was Constantine's theory that, as a supreme Mystery, it might unite his crumbling empire. For it had gloriously maintained its coherence through all the persecutions and the hideous hatreds of its past, and he hoped that Eternal Rome might do the same in this moment of disintegration.

But sheer paganism would not die. The official and sudden accrediting of Christianity could not lift ingrained pagans into a different mental idiom all at once. Therefore paganism dominated essential Christianity by its cultural postulate of magic authority. The priesthood evolved from informal eldership through gradations of aura up to bishops, archbishops, and popes who were far from the unpretentious simplicities of the earliest apostles. The Love Feast of Upper Room fellowship was transformed into the Mass, the miraculous efficacy of which was an exact repetition of the Mystery's own valid formulae. Hairsplitting criteria of dogma were debated about such questions as the inner "hypostases" of the Trinity, the eternal fate of unbaptized infants, the election of the predestined. Heretics sent their imaginations into the stratosphere and returned with wide-eyed Gnosis, mystic information about cosmic ultimates and the hidden God from Whom a long series of divine essences descends, until the last and weakest is the Demiurge who created our world. Excommunications were their reward. Then Augustine built on

Paul's precedent with his own systematic formulation of dogma. Without derogation of Augustine's genius and dramatic personality, the sad truth is that his theories did more harm to simple Christianity than any other individual's since Paul's. Augustine gave momentum to sacramentarian magic and built on it the high structure of esoteric doctrine on which the Councils and the "Angelic Doctor" Thomas Aquinas rested their case. And Rome has accepted this system as final.

(3) The course of history accidentally favored this process of magicizing the Church. The Council of Nicaea (325 A.D.) was called by Constantine to give the whole and variantly spreading Church some homogeneity. For patriarchs or popes, bishops great or small, hermits or metropolitan pontiffs were as their local environment happened to condition them. Although, so to speak, the emperor was senior warden of the church in Rome, the papacies of Constantinople, Jerusalem, Antioch, and Alexandria were of equal authority and accordingly were so commissioned by the assignment of missionary responsibility in their hinterlands. The empire declined. The emperor decamped to Constantinople and left the Roman popes to face the barbarian invasions—which heroically they did. Then Mohammedanism went on the rampage: Alexandria, Jerusalem, and Antioch were conquered and Constantinople was robbed of its terrain. But when the Moslems attempted to pour in through Europe's back door across Spain, up out of the yet unconsidered Gothic domain rose the Frankish kingdom's armies to stop them, and revealed trans-Alpine Europe as a vague barbaric mission field. The spurious "Donation of Constantine" was then produced, which allegedly had bequeathed to the Roman Pope and his successors the supremacy over all other

prelates of the Church and the temporal rulership over vast territories. Although the Roman Church later acknowledged this document to be forged, it served its purpose at the time: the Frankish kings bowed to it and Charlemagne was crowned emperor of the Holy *Roman* Empire by Rome's Pope. Ultramontanism had come to stay as Rome's cardinal claim. Hildebrand made Henry IV grovel at Canossa and established the right to "invest" both emperors and their bishops with insignia of office. Magic authoritarianism was at its zenith.

(4) It is easy to trace what came to pass. When Clovis made his vow that he and his nation would become Christians if he were victorious in battle, and, according to legend, sent his triumphant army splashing through the river while priests baptized them wholesale, it is doubtful whether his warriors emerged from the stream without mental reservations in favor of the heathen faith with which they had waded into the water.

This is symbolic of Europe's "conversion." The mass of the average populace held tenaciously to their inherited dramatic folk customs. The gods of woods and streams and sky, of love and fertility and conquest, were well entrenched. Their seasonal festivals and disciplines were ancestrally cherished. The new priests were natives of the converted areas; they were bred in native customs. They were decidedly amateur at developed Romanism, but they did their best to assimilate it with their indigenous faiths. Blood told. As their ancestors had rung their bells, they rang theirs to ward off storms. They did not deny the existence of the imps and elves and fairies they exorcised from the pre-empted sanctuaries, but they granted them special dells in the forests for their own use. They were *officially* Christian but they still believed in Pan, Diana and Company on the side. The Church met the native faith halfway. "Keep the familiar customs, under Christian names; ban the old names and forbid the observances which will not consent to be synthesized into the compound of nominality; keep the essence and curse the non-co-operators with threats of damnation," said the policymakers. The village priest of Domremy marched seven times (seven is a magic number) around the Fairy Tree, sprinkling it with holy water (what does a ritual formula actually *do* to water's make-up and power?), and reciting from St. John's Gospel (magic book)—and immediately the tree became the Ladies' Tree on which peasants hung their written prayers and offerings. The tree still provided fertility amulets and in its branches Joan of Arc saw her summoning saints.

Gregory the Great warned the later Augustine, who was his missionary to Britain, that barbarians could not arbitrarily be weaned from their old ways. He bade him, "Sprinkle the places of heathen worship with holy water, build altars and place relics upon them. If these temples are well built, it is fitting that the properties of them should be altered, the Devil abolished and the solemnity changed to the service of the true God." "Then," he said, "the Anglo-Saxons may continue their customary festal rites and festivities to the praise of God and be allowed the satisfaction of sense, that they may relish Christianity the better; for unpolished, ignorant people are not to be changed all at once."

Then the process of conflation, accommodation, and synthesis went deep and wide. Idols were forbidden as such, but images of the saints, suspiciously identical, were installed or renamed—and if properly kissed and garlanded they were supposed to possess the same potency. Relics were everywhere. The knucklebones and skulls of fabled saints were said to have healing power. There were enough pieces of the True Cross to make a dozen crosses. Brigid, the Celtic goddess, became St. Bridget; Eostre, Goddess of the Spring, gave her name to Easter and to the rustic rites which banished King Winter and brought in the spring. Since there was no record of the birth date of Jesus it was appropriate to make Christmas the sublimation of the first longer day after the winter solstice, celebrated from primal days for its assurance of the turn of the season, since Christ was "the Sun of Righteousness arising with healing in His wings." And the very stars in their courses astronomically accorded. Druidism added the hung mistletoe's symbolism; the Norsemen gave Yggdrasil, the evergreen Tree of Life; the Saturnalia added gift-giving and Twelfth Night revels; St. Nicholas of Myra inherited the mantle of the jovial King of the Elves out under the aurora borealis; and the Church put the loaf of bread in the manger for a midnight Christ Mass sacrament at the heart of the folk feast.

White magic, stamped with the Church's imprimatur to combat the surviving nature magic (now called black), was exalted; and recalcitrant nature worshipers were condemned. Pan became the Church's devil, pictured with Pan's horns, hoofs, and tail; and out under the moon secret gatherings of his loyal adherents bootlegged his homage with incantations and ecstacy. Diana, the virgin mother of the gods (under whatever name synonymously called), was fiercely forbidden, but Mary, the perpetually virgin Mother of God, was elevated to the Zodiac's apex, her feet upon Diana's crescent moon.

(5) The professional ecclesiasts also profited by terrors of hell, especially toward the year 1000 when the catastrophic end of the world was definitely expected. The prelates as-

sured their people that Peter had the keys of heaven and hell and had deputized the papacy to act for him on earth. So the only hope of escaping eternal damnation or of shortening Purgatory was in obedience to the Church's ordinances to keep in sacramental good standing. Confession and absolution would bring instantaneous cleansing. The Mass was "opus operatum," that is, a ceremony which changed the spiritual status of the congregation even apart from its attention to or comprehension of the liturgy. Excommunication would bring a horrible fate, hideous beyond imagining. The melodrama of excommunication was direfully based on the credulity that by its magic curse the Church could reach over into eternity and ordain it unending tortures. The dread of aeons of fiery agony under the pitchforks of demons was enough to turn to jelly the spines of the timorous. Even Henry IV crumpled at the menace of this when Hildebrand mentioned "anathema maranatha."

Imagine the scene of excommunication: The great bell of the minster tolls as if for a funeral. The church is hung with black, inside and out. The congregation scarcely breathing, the bishop and black-robed clergy mount the chancel steps, holding lighted torches. The culprit's name is called and the fell sentences are thundered: "Let him be cursed in the city and cursed in the field; cursed in his granary and his harvest and his children; as Dathan and Abiram were swallowed up by the gaping earth, so may Hell swallow him; and even as today we quench these torches, so may the light of his life be quenched to all eternity unless he do repent." Whereat all the priests crash their torches to the stones and tread them out!

No wonder the indulgences to build St. Peter's were so avidly bought. For Tetzel is said to have promised, "When

your coins go clink in Peter's box the gates of Hell swing
wide and he for whom your Mass is said goes free." He may
have overshot his instructions when he advertised that indulgences could be had for sins of those in Purgatory, for
sins not yet absolved, or that, for alluring sins not yet committed, the saving merit of Christ could be had in advance!
But even if he did exceed his instructions, where is the flaw
in his logic, granted his axiom? It was on indulgences that
Martin Luther broke with the papacy. The Reformation,
preceded by stray individual martyred protesters, was on.
But, we repeat, it is not *finished*.

CHAPTER THREE

Roman Catholicism

It is not intelligent to be an anti-Roman fanatic. Religious bigotry is indecent. But a mature analyst of our present era should feel objective concern about the faith and polity of the Roman Church.

Mr. Paul Blanshard has caused a stir by his three books: *American Freedom and Catholic Power; Communism, Democracy, and Catholic Power;* and *The Irish and Catholic Power*. His documented evidence of Roman Catholic power in the present world situation has been so convincing that, despite Roman Catholic endeavors to suppress or vilify it, he has done a great service to our society. Yet there are those who nevertheless disagree with his initial statement which reads, "The Catholic problem, as I see it, is not primarily a religious problem. It is an institutional and political problem. It is a matter of the use and abuse of power by an organization that is not only a church but a state within a state and a state above a state."[1] The mistake seems to be in the words "not primarily." Granted the thorough, inclusive, and detailed exposition of the present Roman Catholic program, the theory on which it is based makes the Church's practice derivative. *It is the Roman Catholic religion itself which is the dynamic of all Roman Catholic activity.* The institutional and political phenomena of the Church only manifest the doctrinal assumptions which are their inspiration. The Catholic problem *is primarily* a religious problem.

[1]Paul Blanshard, *American Freedom and Catholic Power* (Boston, 1949), pp. 3-4.

To discuss modern Catholicism without a study of its theological dogmas is like discussing the works of a watch without considering the mainspring.

The judgment that the doctrines of the papacy and its Church are unsound is not to accuse its adherents of conscious hypocrisy or guile. Most Roman Catholics are wholeheartedly sincere. And surely their lives are as decent as the lives of any other religious group or of commonsense independents. And the sacerdotal professionals who administer affairs from the Vatican down to the humblest village or city parish are seldom aware of the irrational foundations of their system. They are conditioned by inheritance and routine. Their faith runs in a rut worn through centuries of acceptance. Their prescribed piety makes them deaf to all challenges to examine the warrant of authority. The growth of doctrine has been so gradual that they are not aware of its evolution. Held by training and corporate insistence, emotionally moved by august ceremonial, seduced into awe of the mysteries which are proclaimed as the truth beyond reason, the faithful are bound fast. Catechism answers still suffice to move their subconsciousness toward implicit credulity. Authority has immunized them from the contagion of doubt.

According to Catholic definition, faith is "the act of the intellect assenting to Divine Truth owing to the movement of the will, which is itself moved by the Grace of God."[2] In other words, the will to assent is a submission of the mind. That definition is often given with the added maxim that the harder it is to submit, the more is the merit. Catholic dogma rests on the assertion that reason needs to be supplemented by revelation, and that revelation comes only to the

---

[2]Thomas Aquinas, *De Veritate*, II, II, Q. IV, A. 2; also in *Catholic Encyclopedia*, Vol. 5, p. 756.

Church, which is thereby authorized to regulate the faith of its members. "Revelation means that the Supreme Truth has spoken to man and revealed to him truths which are not in themselves evident to the human mind. We must either reject Revelation altogether or accept it by faith; that is, *we must submit our intellect to Truth, which we cannot understand but which comes to us on Divine Authority.*"[3] There it is—magic authority!

If such submission is made, Catholics need not and even should not think for themselves. Like the peasants bowing before Louis the Magnificent they need only ask, "Good Master, what are our convictions?"

The Roman Catholic Church dictates accordingly, with the aura of that revelation which is monopolized magic. The papacy rests its case on this. Used consistently, resoundingly, with sufficient dogmatism and with ever-new articulation, the technique of manipulated truth has succeeded—with its own people.

Outsiders are baffled at Catholic acceptance of such a doctrine as this: "The Eternal Father, who revealed to Simon Bar Jona the mystery of the divine Sonship of Christ . . . had from all eternity predestined the fisherman of Bethsaida for his singular office.

"And Christ Himself only fulfilled the will of His Father when, promising and conferring the primacy, He used expressions which were to fix forever the uniqueness of Peter's privileged position. . . . For . . . it is certain that He wished to entrust to Peter and to his successors the guidance and government of the Universal Church and the treasures of Truth and Grace of His work of Redemption."[4]

---

[3]*Catholic Encyclopedia*, Vol. 5, p. 753; italics mine.

[4]Pope's address to the College of Cardinals, May 1944.

Claiming to possess secrets beyond all that is recorded in the Gospels, the Church asserts that it has the function of error-free teaching. "Out of such effort has arisen the structure we call Catholic theology," says the Pope. "And through the centuries this theological effort has been fashioned by the Church into a light for the minds of men as well as a weapon to protect the precious heritage of Revelation. As the Body of Christ, the living voice of Christ *is* in the Church by the Divine Will and Promise. Her teaching office is divinely instituted and divinely guaranteed."[5]

The pope has authority to define dogmas ex cathedra, without recorded evidence. In such utterances he is "infallible." There seems to be no limit to the extraordinary dogmas he and the Vatican can fashion. Witness the Holy Year's proclamation of the Assumption of Mary. On November 1, 1950, in the presence of five hundred bishops and thirty-five ermined cardinals, he staged the pronouncement. Sitting on a throne before the central gate of St. Peter's, flanked by Michelangelo's Swiss Guard, amid the fanfare of golden trumpets and "Tu es Petro" by the Sistine Choir, the mitred Pope "received" the ritual petition that the dogma be proclaimed. Whereupon, through a microphone, he enunciated the said dogma that the soul of the Mother of God, ever-virgin and exempt from original sin, went into heaven at her death, and her body was also taken up into heaven on the wings of angels, and reunited with her soul, so that, without bodily corruption, she now sits at the right hand of her Son in heaven, crowned its Queen forever. And lest anyone balk, his Holiness made it a heresy to question this: "The Presence of Mary in soul and body in Heaven is a God-

[5]Encyclical *Humani Generis*, August 12, 1950.

revealed Truth.   Henceforth if anyone presumes to think otherwise, let him know that in his judgment he stands condemned, has suffered shipwreck in faith and has separated himself from the Church's Unity."

And the bells of Rome joyously pealed out this, the Holy Year's crowning glory, to the millions of pilgrims accumulating their plenary indulgences by participating in the jubilee.

The submission of the mind is indeed difficult for objective non-Catholics to understand.   Yet in almost every stage of its development, sincere and devoted servants of the institution have been its extenders.   They have simply worked from an unreal premise, the premise of magic.

The craving for drama is a universal appetite.   The impressiveness of good pageantry is unquestionable.   But its exploitation turns drama into melodrama and pageantry into ostentation.   It is then a kind of profanity.   The Roman Catholic Church uses all the arts to awe its children into homage.   The accumulated resources of theatrical sensation, rich liturgy, musical genius, Gothic architecture, and hierarchical officials are drawn upon with a total emotional effectiveness which forces even non-conformists to recognize its strength.   Add to this the prestige of world-wide unity and of historic continuity through the centuries (according to that Church's version of historicity), plus the promise of safety and grace after death, and it is no wonder that millions genuflect.

The doctrine of saving grace channeled solely through the Roman Catholic Church ties in with the Church's claims to the "treasury of merit" and to "transubstantiation in the Mass."

Even among average Catholics there is confusion about the workings of supererogatory merit and the sacrifice of the

Cross. The theory begins with the charitable concession to human nature that there is an attainable quantum of goodness which could be enough to save one's soul, but above this quantum it is also thinkable that one can do more than is required. Works of supererogation create merit not personally needed. Merit makes saints. Since the saints do not need their overplus, that merit goes into the "treasury of merit" which is administered through the Church. If you and I are (Catholic) sinners our quantum of goodness is so much in arrears that we can never lift ourselves to par, try as hard as we may. What shall we do then? Mother Church's solution is simple: if we cast ourselves upon her mercy, make our confession to the priest, perform the prescribed penance, and make our Communion, the priest's absolution and the Mass put to our account and into our life the necessary amount of merit, drawn from the Church's store. Furthermore, in his sinless humanity Jesus did not need the merit of the Cross for himself. His death on Calvary created such an illimitable fund of merit that the Church to which he transmitted it has an inexhaustible treasury of it on which to draw.

Whenever the Mass is celebrated, the sacrifice of Christ is repeated and, each time, merit is drawn from the ever-sufficient treasury.

Transubstantiation is said to accomplish this. The *conversio substantialis* allows the "accidents" of bread and wine to remain, but "according to the purpose of the Almighty the *substance* of the bread and wine departs in order to make room for the Body and Blood of Christ. The pre-existent Christ assumes a new, sacramental mode of being. The conversion of the total substance is the express doctrine of the Church."[6] The real presence of the Crucified is not only of

---

[6]Council of Trent, Sess. XIII, Can. II.

his body and blood but of his humanity, his soul, and his divinity. When the body is separate from the blood "the mystical slaying thus approaches nearer to a real death and the absolute sacrificial moment of the Mass receives confirmation." The Holy Eucharist is therefore necessary for salvation.

This raises the point of indulgences which, in their gradation up to plenary indulgences, seem evasions of the hard work of character. In the Holy Year advertisements, the plenary proffer was held out to pilgrims who, after confession and Communion, would visit stipulated churches in the Eternal City and recite a few prayers. If the Rosary is said before the Holy Sacrament's monstrance, if the scapular of the Dominicans is kissed (one hundred days indulgence), if the Litany of Mary is recited so-and-so (three hundred), if certain special intercessions are said so many times (a year's remittance) . . .

The Scholastic explanation of indulgences is subtle. "An Indulgence is a partial or total remission of the temporal punishment which remains because of sin after its guilt has been taken away by priestly Absolution."[7]

It must be understood that the guilt of sin thrusts the culprit out of the privileges of grace. Absolution only puts the sinner back into the field of operations of grace. Penance and absolution are effective only thus far; punishment still has to be worked out. But there is merit which can be used by the Church to substitute for a given amount of that punishment, according to the degree of indulgence. The indulgenced person may be living or in Purgatory. (Souls in hell cannot be indulgenced for they are finally damned to its literal flames.) A plenary indulgence will even bring imme-

---

[7]*Catholic Encyclopedia,* under Indulgences.

diate release to a soul in Purgatory, provided that soul is opened to grace by the "satisfaction" wrought by the intercessor. One longs to be a Socrates and challenge such "revelation" with his "How do you know?"

Indulgences are easily abused. Mention has been made of Tetzel's salesmanship which touched off Martin Luther's expulsion. Similar abuse is also too frequent today. Archbishop Sinnot of Winnipeg illustrated this when under date of March 1, 1944, he appealed for Catholic mothers to enroll their G.I. sons who were at the front as Perpetual Members of the Society for the Propagation of the Faith—at forty dollars in easy payments, to "insure the Boy's safety as far as we can do so, his safety in time and eternity." The Archbsihop also wrote, "What better guarantee for any boy exposed to all the hazards of war! A guarantee that, should he be killed, he will go at once to his Maker, to be with Him for all eternity. A guarantee, *should it be God's will* [*sic*], that he will return to his dear mother and to those who love him."[8]

All collateral dogmas are secondary to that of sacramental grace. For instance, the patron saint, to whom "God in consequence of His infallible promise owes a supernatural reward," seems to be a kind of celestial lobbyist. St. Christopher medals hang in countless automobiles to ward off accidents and are in purses of countless travelers, as are images of St. Joseph for good luck. Wafers stamped with the image of St. Joseph are given as medicine. A gift to St. Anthony helps in the discovery of lost articles. St. Rita helps sick people to recovery and grateful acknowledgments for her favors are given publicity in newspaper personal columns.

---

[8]*Christian Century*, Vol. 61, July 12, 1944, pp. 823-4; *New Republic*, Vol. 3, same date. See also *The Witness*, June 22, 1944, pp. 8-9. Italics mine.

Local saints give a neighborly touch. Bernadette sponsors Lourdes; Mother Cabrini, canonized in 1946, gives America its domestic saint. Pius X is now to be canonized; reports of miracles by his influence since his beatification in 1951 have been received at the Vatican in sufficient volume to justify this further step. But of all the saints there are none who approach the Virgin, who makes appearances to peasants in trance and becomes variously Our Lady of the Rosary and Our Lady of Fatima, where she predicted the conversion of Russia if enough prayer and penance were brought to bear. For, Bishop Sheen[9] is accustomed to argue, God Almighty seems too remote and abashing as the Sovereign of all creation for humble human beings to approach directly, and Jesus is so supernatural as a Person of the Trinity that the tender Mother of God provides the most natural liaison with the Eternal. She is the All-Mother as well as the bearer of the Savior. Immaculately conceived and thereby prenatally exempt from the original sin which is in the genes of all other descendants of Adam, she nevertheless has her human side and can be touched by her foster children's yearnings.

Rome says it is the only true Church, that because of its "monopoly of grace" no other churches are valid. Pamphlet racks in Catholic vestibules are filled with booklets which reiterate that "The Catholic Church is the only organization authorized by God to teach religious truth and to conduct public religious worship. Consequently Catholics hold that any creed which differs from that of the Catholic Church is

---

[9]A footnote recognition of Bishop Sheen's influence is in order. He is the greatest converter of prominent persons, the most finished and consummate actorial artist, and the most suave propagandist the Roman Church has in the East. His preaching, his books, and his television program are remarkable, if studied, persuasion. With his marvelous hands, his mesmeric eyes, and his resonant voice, his cleverness becomes seductive. The Church does well to capitalize him for its chief apologist.

erroneous, and that any religious organization which is separated from the Catholic Church lacks the approval and
authorization of God. The very existence of any other church
is opposed to the command of Christ that all men should
join His one Church. From this it follows that, as far as
God's law is concerned, no one has a real right to accept any
religion save the Catholic religion. . . . God has imposed
on all men the obligation to accept and practice Catholicism."[10]

*Therefore to the Church any accommodation to the laws
of a democratic state which grants civil rights to other faiths
is strictly an interim policy.* The plausible rationalization
which the Catholic Church gives for this temporary compromise with the state is that a state which allowed no civil
privileges to non-Catholics would force possibly hypocritical
membership on their part when only sincere conviction is
desired. Meanwhile the "invincibly erroneous conscience"
of the non-Catholic gives him no genuine right to accept that
religion in opposition to God's command.

Of late there has been a more open defiance of this interim
policy. Statement after statement hews more closely to the
assertion that the Catholic Church should be the established
church of the state. The recent statement by the Catholic
cardinals, archbishops, and bishops of the United States at
their annual meeting in November, 1952, flat-footedly defies
what it names as the secularism of our society, by which is
meant the separation of church and state, leaving the state
devoid of true religion. It will be well to quote a few of the
background paragraphs which lead up to the practical issue
of religion in education. Read them and weigh their assertion

---

[10]Francis J. Connell, "Freedom of Worship—The Catholic Position," pamphlet
issued by the Paulist Press, New York, Imprimatur Francis J. Spellman, D.D.

that revelation is *the* essential to religion—which revelation is Catholic.

While civic authority may have its immediate source in the consent of the governed, that authority must be recognized as coming ultimately from Him upon Whom all men depend.

In the measure to which the state has excluded religion it has shown a tendency to become an instrument of tyranny. The irreligious state sets itself up in the place of God. It demands an absolute loyalty such as can be claimed only by Truth itself.

Those who follow this secular way of life distort and blot out our religious traditions and seek to remove all influence of religion from public life. Their main efforts are centered on the divorce of religion from education. [But remember, there is only one religion.]

One of the constant dangers to the religious spirit in a country is the tendency . . . to be content with the great religious truths of the natural order which can be known by unaided human reason. . . . They are but part of a religious truth. It is through supernatural faith alone that man comes to the knowledge of religious truth in its fullness. To attain to his destiny, therefore, man needs not merely the truths which reason can discover, he needs also the truths which Christ revealed: *he needs the Church which Christ has established . . .;* only the life of Christian faith can guarantee to man in his present state the moral life; *and the Christian life is lived in its entirety only through the one true Church of Christ.*[11]

Here is the unequivocal declaration of an interim's ending, if the Church can abrogate our secular state. After all, it is consistent with papal declarations. Leo XIII, in his encyclical on human liberties, laid down the principle, "Since the profession of one religion is necessary for the State, that religion must be professed which alone is true. This religion, therefore, the rulers of the State must protect and preserve. It is quite unlawful to demand, defend or grant unconditional freedom of thought, of speech, of writing or of worship."

[11]Italics mine.

Such itemization of Catholic infringements of our democratic system as Mr. Blanshard documents is alarming in the nth degree, but it must be remembered that it is the Roman Catholic religion as such which inspires all of its policies.

The self-evident fact is that the Roman Church, because of its insistence that it alone is authorized by divine fiat, not only does not but *cannot* subscribe to democratic principles or practices. The proclaimed charter underlying all the Vatican's diplomatic and political program is that it magically has been given jurisdiction over everything human. No bona fide proof is or can be offered which will stand up under impartial scrutiny; yet, uttered with sufficient repetition and cumulative institutional pretentiousness, it demands total submission and allegiance. All the gradual and alarming encroachments on democracy come from the Church's theocratic, exclusivist ideology. Ultramontanism is its ineradicable ideal.[12]

---

[12]Among many other instances of ultramontanist activity there is perhaps no better example of special pleading attempting to vindicate the magical inerrancy of God-constituted Catholicism than its arrant misrepresentation of Cardinal Stepinac. The reverberating cries that Tito was guilty of blasphemous impiety in persecuting a saintly apostle of the truth have tried to drown out the fact, once boasted by the Church but now hushed, that Stepinac was a collaborationist with the Nazis in their campaign to take over Croatia and make it a Catholic state. The documented record of the Catholic terrorist organization, the Ustashi, and its too successful endeavor to impose a Nazi-Fascist regime under the quislings, Pavelich and Kvaternic, deeply involves the cardinal who welcomed them with open arms. Although—or because—the Greek Orthodox Church is by far the majority church in Yugoslavia, the Ustashi carried on the forcible "conversion" of the surviving population. Nearly 70,000 of the 805,000 Jews were killed or forced to flee and their property was confiscated; 240,000 Serbs were forced to "become Catholics" on pain of death, and those who resisted were shot or stabbed, their bodies tumbled into mass graves And this was in the diocese in which Aloysius Stepinac was the supreme authority and the military vicar of the Ustashi armed forces These Ustashis were so sure that the "New Order" would triumph that they preserved the record of their own crimes At his trial, Stepinac did not deny the evidence produced, but he pleaded that he had been morally justified because he had acted for a Catholic Croatia against the threat of Communism That the Vatican can rationalize cardinal's robes for such a man is in line with the magical theory of the infallibility of the Church.

Here in America, particularly in the United States (which is now reputed to provide 90 per cent of its finances), the Roman Church is moving beyond interim compromises with democracy. With the tide running out from under the papacy in Europe, the most important field is here.

We may think of two domestic illustrations of magical authority: censorship and the proscription of birth control. Censorship means the suppression of personal decisions by the arbitrary decision of authority. The Roman Church's censorship walls out everything which endangers its dogmas. Freedom of thought is denied.

The Index Librorum Prohibitorum rules that "all men are forbidden to read books that are contrary to faith in God, good moral conduct and Christian virtue." (By "faith" Roman doctrine is meant.) Past condemnations are irrevocable for a surprising list of great literature. All of Dumas except *Monte Cristo* and all the works of Balzac, Stendahl, George Sand, Zola, and Voltaire are included. Gibbon's *Decline and Fall* is interdict, and so are the works of Kant, Locke, Hume, Descartes, Spencer, and many other standard philosophers. Most scientific writing is disallowed, save for favored students who can get an official permit. Censorship also clamps down on motion pictures, television, the theater.

Roman Catholic efforts to impose the Church's criteria beyond the Catholic membership on the entire citizenry, however, cannot be more clearly exhibited than in the campaign against birth control. The nub of the Roman Catholic position which denies private decision in this most intimately personal relationship is that "the processes of Nature as God has established them" must not be interfered with, even to save the life of a mother or to prevent the dissolution of a decent home.

In matters of faith the Roman Catholic Church may have authority to dictate to its own membership, as far as that membership is content to submit. But the magical authority should not extend—by force or by pressure—to those who do not accept it. The springhead of Roman Catholicism's ramifying cabal is its initial and fundamental premise of magic prerogative. The danger is in the imposition of this on others.

CHAPTER FOUR

The Problems of Judaism

Note what the title of this chapter is *not*. It is not the Jewish Problem: it is the Problems of Judaism within itself. Anti-Semitism, with its roots in medieval "Christian" bigotry, in the main may not be consciously religious now and the Jew's anti-Gentilism may have less solely religious bias, but inherited subconsciousness still works both ways. It is in the Jewish genes that "Yisroel" is the "Champion of God"; and, although the "chosen people" is a poor translation of *"am segullah,"* it is emotionally natural for most Jews to feel that Jewry is a "treasure people." For all Jews who think of their blood, "Israel is the wick, God the flame and the Law the oil" of Jewry's sacred lamp. It is therefore imperative to remember that the total complex of Jewish problems is indelibly religious, even where religion seems not to enter in. And the birthright is "revelational"—therefore miraculous.

Western Judaism parallels the Christian Church in its own predicaments and trends. Judaism has the familiar tug of war between its literalists, its half-liberals, its more complete liberals, and its indifferent secularists. Yet there is a special difference from the Christian Church in that the pulls in Judaism are even more intense and from wider extremes. This is because its ancient formulation, so many centuries prior to Christianity, was in an Israel in which church and state were one in a single meticulous, authoritarian system, and because its modern conditions are *in* but not entirely *of* a Gentile society which in the main tolerates but does not sympathetically comprehend the Jewish character.

Judaism includes the Orthodox, the Reformed, and the Conservative wings. Because of the congregational polity of the synagogue system, there are almost no reliable statistics of membership. Even the Jewish Year Book ventures very few. Since any ten adult males can form a synagogue, since a synagogue may even function without a rabbi, and since a rabbi is not a sacerdotal priest but rather a teacher, almost a layman, there are only general groupings. Apparently, of the five million Jews in the United States, about a hundred thousand are Reformed, a hundred and fifty thousand are Conservative, and a larger number than the others together are Orthodox. Non-affiliated Jews, probably secular in mood, are still more numerous.

All three schools hold the Torah, the prophets and the calendar of feasts and fasts in common, and regard the Talmud in varying degrees of awe. All accept the Torah as in some way "revealed," as miraculously given by Jehovah. The classic statement is that "Moses received the Torah at Sinai and transmitted it to Joshua, Joshua to the elders, the elders to the prophets and the prophets to the men of the Great Synagogue." [1]

The Torah has been the "portable fatherland" of the Jew. It has preserved the Jew longer than any state in Israel has preserved its citizens. No higher criticism has destroyed its vital sanctity, no ritual Sabbatarianism has quite smothered its supernatural *mana*.

Orthodox Judaism is as nearly what it was in the seventh century B.C. as is practicable in this alien day. The *mitz-woth*—the sacred commandments, precepts, the perform-

[1] Aboth 1:1.

ance of minutely detailed ceremonial duties—make life according to prescription the only salvation. The six hundred
and thirteen *mitzwoth* are taken as symbolic of the number
of bones in the human body, plus the number of days in the
year, so that the pious Jew is to observe the Law with every
bone in his body every day of the year. The religion of the
Orthodox soon grows to be unconcerned with spiritualities;
it is a regimen of laws, traditions, customs and rituals, a pious
sorcery to bring the Messiah and the millennium for the children of Abraham.

When a black-bearded, long-coated Orthodox rabbi, side
curls worn in front of his ears, skull cap beneath his broad-
brimmed felt hat, sits in a subway train reading a rabbinic
Hebrew book of Mishnah selections, fellow passengers may
well speculate on how he can still apply the ancient pattern
in the East Side of today. Down in his cross-street synagogue
next Saturday he will don his prayer shawl and stand before
the open Ark, intoning immemorial prayers and being answered by the cantor's antiphons exactly in the vibrato of the
Babylonian exiles. For him there is no such thing as an
evolving revelation. No Second Moses will ever arise to bring
a new edition of the Law. The divine revelation, miraculously given to the elect, is complete, binding, and final in its
written and its oral form. There is no uncertainty in the
mind of the devout Orthodoxist; every aspect of existence is
covered—except that the ancient articulation needs present-
day application. For instance, at Passover time, is chocolate
kosher if made with the new soybean butter? Soybeans are
not in Leviticus! Does the Sabbath injunction against light-
ing lamps apply to electric switches? Does the limitation of
a Sabbath Day's journey (on foot) determine the mileage of
an automobile ride (sitting in comfort)? What of a double-

ring marriage ceremony, now indicative of the equality of
man and woman, when the Law stipulates a single, jewelless
ring as the token of the symbolic purchase of the bride? Just
as the Pharisees once planned that there should never be a
human situation for which there was not a statutory ordi-
nance in advance, so the punctilious servant of the Law continues Sabbatarian hairsplittings about two-handed versus
one-handed knots, vinegar for food versus vinegar as tooth-
ache medicine, the width of the border of his prayer shawl,
the number of threads times knots in its tassels, and the tiny
parchment in the phylactery.

Small wonder it is that the doctrinally inured Jew shud-
ders at what Christians have made of Jesus. As Paul too
well knew then, Israel recoils from the doctrine of a crucified
Messiah. The creedal idea of Jesus as the pre-existent, incarnate second Person of the Trinity is unthinkable to a Jew,
for Judaism has unalterably affirmed that there can be no
special sonship of the One and Only Jehovah. To his fierce
monotheism the whole dogma of the atonement is absurd
and blasphemous. And, sad to realize, the conduct of Christ's
disciples throughout the Inquisitional past, on and on to
modern anti-Semitism, has not recommended their nominal
faith. Orthodox Jews cannot even be open-minded toward
the inclusion of Jesus as one of the prophets, for in their eyes
he was heretical, supra-national, and subversive of authority,
and he paid the penalty reserved for the most heinous rebels,
a penalty so defiling that only "unclean" Romans were used
for the execution of its vengeance upon him. Christianity
is abhorrent to the dogmatic Jew. It affronts his whole psyche
and his ritual magic.

Christians must therefore have a new birth of charity for
the ideology of Jewry, even in its most inflexible traditional-

ism. The rich drama of its feasts and fasts is mystically
noble. A sensitive Gentile may well feel a tremor of sympathy at the veneration of the sacred scrolls when the Ark is
opened, at the Hanukkah "Mooz-tsur" hymn of the Rock of
Ages, at the murmur of the Kaddish intercession for the coming of God's kingdom, and, most of all, as the "Shema"
seems to echo from Sinai itself, "Hear, O Israel, the Lord
our God, the Lord is One!" The epic timbre is electric. In
the cycle of holy days the emotion of their observance pulses
across the centuries. In imagination one may listen to the
ram's horn of New Year's and the anguished chant of Atonement's "Kol Nidre," or vicariously feel the glow of the Passover Seder in the Jewish home. If only meticulous obedience
to a microscopic directive were not taken by the Orthodox
as a prayerful sorcery to guarantee the Messianic kingdom's
reversal of the present supremacy of the *Hagoim* in the
world!

The tense issue of Zionism is bound up with this Old Testament literalism. Orthodox Jews are likely to be nationalists,
working and praying for a sovereign state in Palestine. Apart
from the poignant humanitarian grounds for the movement,
the dream of the national restoration of the Promised Land
is eagerly pursued, that a world capital of Jehovah's Own
may be contrived with the temple as its focus, where the
Messiah can be enthroned to judge and rule the earth after
the Great Assize. It is hoped that the creation of the Zionist
state will therefore stop the rapid process of assimilation and
disintegration in an alien society. Outside of Palestine, the
Orthodox Jew feels he is in exile. The prayers of the Wail-
ing Wall have always been for "the nation Israel for the
land of Israel through the Torah of Israel." Can they be
answered?

Orthodox Judaism is *the* problem with which the more liberal Jews have to wrestle. Reformed Judaism swings the pendulum of faith to the opposite end of the Jewish arc. It is committed to rethinking ancestral tenets, to continuing their liberalization and spiritualization. It demands the right of free evaluation and of discovering the new truth, by evolution from the past. The true authority for Reformed Jewry is not a supernatural revelation to Moses but the on-going spirit of Israel. Every age writes a chapter in the Covenant. Truth is not static. Rigid external authority is to be distrusted. The formulae of the Torah are to be screened by common sense; for instance, dietary regimen can be disregarded. The prophets are relied upon as examples of moral courage, advancing true righteousness. The expectation of a personally embodied Messiah is replaced in Reformed Judaism by the tenacious hope of an age-to-be when the world struggle shall at last have brought a reign of decency, peace, liberty, justice, and good will.

Specific reforms stem from this liberalism. Vernacular, as well as Hebrew, is used in worship. The Prayer Book is revised to eliminate anthropomorphic phrasing, the physical resurrection of the dead, nationalistic ideals, and the claim that "Israel is the chosen of the Almighty." Ceremonies are modified, vitalized, and simplified. The Sabbath is lifted out of negative legalism. The religious equality of women is made plain in marriage and in synagogue worship.

But Reformed Judaism has brought a lack of cohesive unity in the faith. The democratic process, temporarily at least, stimulates adventures in liberty, not always evolutionary but sometimes revolutionary. Therefore Conservative Judaism has tried a middle road between ancient and modern. The thesis of the Conservatives is "positive historic Judaism."

Tradition is not to be lightly cast aside; for any usage or institution acquired through the centuries has integral meaning, and its sanctity is to be reckoned with. The authority of the Torah comes from its spiritual meaning for Jewry. The central axiom of Conservatism is "an enlightened scepticism combined with a staunch conservatism, which is not devoid of a mystical touch."[2] Conservatism stays inside the canon of the Law. Change, it says, must be within its limits.

Conservative Judaism, therefore, adds its influence to Orthodox Zionism. To Conservatives, although Judaism is an international nation, its homeland is Palestine. In Palestine can be preserved and clarified for all Jewry everywhere the pattern of national folkways, customs, language, sentiment and loyalties, the civilization which is Judaism.

Conservatism represents a compromise with fundamentalism, a retrograde movement away from true liberalism. Magic has again forced negation of clear-minded realism. Except for Reformed Judaism, magic has retained its complete or semi-potent grip on the Jewish faith.

Brazen religionlessness is perhaps more shocking when it is paraded by Jews than when Gentiles boast of it. That shock must be because we unconsciously feel that the stewards of so noble and courageous a birthright have sold it for a mess of merely secular pottage. Somehow, to their credit, we subconsciously expect that Jews will retain the flavor of the rich antiquities of faith of their race. With considerable shame it is to be admitted that in contrast to Judaism, the nominally Christian world has so far grown into unconcern about religion that it is not perturbed on its own religious score. It is a kind of compliment if Jews are presupposed to be in earnest about their faith. Yet out of our five million

---

[2]Solomon Schechter, *Studies in Judaism* (Philadelphia, 1896), Series I, p. xvii.

Jews, the non-synagogue majority is probably 60-plus percent. This majority must not be permitted to deteriorate into attrition and gross materialism, into forgetfulness of the genius of all the magnificent Jewish philosophers, poets, musicians, jurists, public benefactors, and other sons of the prophets who are of the birthright. Such a spiritual loss would leave everyone everywhere who cherishes human greatness, immeasurably impoverished. The stewardship of such a brave religion, although that religion now deserves modernization and a rejection of narrow doctrine and magic ritual, is infinitely stirring and precious to the world.

CHAPTER FIVE

The Sin of Sectarianism

The killing blight on the orthodox Christian Church is sectarianism. Despite its doctrinal self-assurance, any denomination which vaunts its superior or sole validity against the claims of other denominations is a victim of this blight.

All the orthodox churches are cousins, whether or not they acknowledge their kinship in faith. They are members of one generic family, whose differences are domestic—rival hairsplittings over administrational set-up and creedal interpretations of a shared body of belief. It is proper to speak of the Christian *Church,* for the subdivisions inside it are on the basis of individualistic egoisms which in comparison with the main thesis of traditional Christianity are insignificant. Whether a given denomination, local church, or single member is liberal or conservative inside this Holy Catholic Church (Catholic in this sense meaning all-inclusive), whether Protestant or Roman Catholic or of a fringe communion, the same axioms are acknowledged—of the Trinity, the divinity of Jesus as Lord, Savior, and God, the efficacy of the sacraments, of salvation through the Church, and of the Bible's plenary inspiration.

Outside the pale, where dogmatic Christianity draws the line of demarcation, are the unorthodox groups which cannot acknowledge these axioms. Even the poor relations inside the family group, down to the least substantial and most pathetic of them, look on such organizations as the American Unitarian Association, the Humanist Fellowship, and the

Ethical Culture Society as no churches at all because of their heretical abandonment of the so-called Christian criteria. The World Council of Churches and the National Council of the Churches of Christ in America bar them from fellowship with a sanctimonious shudder. Christianity, dogmatically defined, is so coherent a tradition that its name has come to mean a specific code of theology tied to a magic Christ, instead of a sharing in the simple faith that Jesus himself had, taught, and lived. Because of this presumption of the Christian name as a trademark of the ecclesiastically developed doctrine, no Samaritan liberal, even if he implicitly holds the religion of Jesus, can now answer that he is a Christian or even that he believes in God, without first inquiring in what sense the names are being used. To be Christian in spirit is not enough to qualify; one must be a Christian in the Church's sense, or be a pariah.

Even Christian liberals inside the pale who peer over the fence which confines doctrinal Christianity, wistfully eyeing the wide green field beyond, are nevertheless still within the Church. The mutually excoriating, the mutually ignoring, or the Platonically tolerant denominations are allied and akin; canonical Christianity is the common denominator of all orthodoxy.

The orthodox Church is like a tree with wide-spreading roots which draw ideas from pre-Christian subsoil. Its planted acorn was the life of the Son of Man. The tree sprang up into A. D. history in a slender single trunk. The Eastern Orthodox Church separated from that trunk. At the Reformation the main trunk divided into two limbs, the Protestant and Catholic. The Protestant limb subdivided into branches, the denominations (how often, and how accurately, a denomination is spoken of as a branch of the Church), then into their own parochial twigs and ultimately to the seasonal leaves and blossoms which are their members. To this day the Protestant communions perpetuate from the Reformation these divergent forkings, the Eastern Orthodox its few, but the Roman its undivided shaft. It is the Protestant limb we are now considering.

When the rebellion against papal domination broke out in the Reformation, the question was how far back in the Church's evolutionary course the reformers must go to find the form of organization which fitted their principles. Zwingli and his adherents went farthest to the inherent right of the individual congregation to fix its own covenant and government: thus the Congregationalist and Baptist polity ever since. Calvin did not go quite so far. He felt that more co-ordination was expedient; he therefore built his denomination on the significance of the presbyters. The elders would transmit its ideal and ordain its disciplines. Thus the Presbyterian communions. Luther and the Dutch and Scandinavian and English reformers stopped short of reliance on the presbyters and, being nationalist-minded, leveled off at the episcopate, which was forbidden to be papal yet was vested with the prestige of the established state church and its regional functions. Therefore the Episcopal churches of the "Apostolic Succession."

All denominations are built on the *theory* that in each one the membership has a unanimous mind as to its faith and order. In proportion as broader creedal generalities are reduced to detailed articulation, the resultant confessions, covenants and articles inevitably muster fewer and fewer adherents who can fit their Procrustean bed. Brought down to subtle nuances of dogma and commanded to sign on the dotted line of exact conformity, few people think identically. Constitutions and bylaws have been drafted; bishops, moderators, conventions, and sessions have developed "Episcopitis"; disciplines have been thundered, shibboleths have been elevated to password standards, and the inevitable result has been the increase of non-conformity rather than the reverse. Hard and fast dogma just cannot confine spontaneous thinking. Illiberality is the earmark of the dogmatic ideal: it is the typical characteristic of the power complex. Even though the elaborate geometry of the Athanasian Creed's Trinitarian diagram may be pre-Reformation in statement, its inherited spirit of intolerance animates all unregenerate sectarianism to this day:

> Whosoever will be saved: before all things it is necessary that he hold the [Catholic] faith . . . which faith, except everyone do keep whole and undefiled, without doubt he shall perish everlastingly.

It may be objected that the liberals within the churches are not truly represented by such outmoded formulas, although they do not overtly resent their imposition by authority. Be that as it may, is there any denying that these very formulas are still the unchanged official criteria of their respective communions? Brought to book and challenged, these broader-minded individuals would have to concede that the norm of their denomination is a Mede and Persian law which altereth not, and they must admit that its terms are fixed.

The moment has come when a drastic test must be met. Liberals of all denominations are now actually closer to each other than they are to the conservatives in their own communions. Correspondingly, the conservatives of all denominations are closer to each other than to the liberals in their own groups. So far as temperament and general attitude classify the churchmen of our day, the real division between them is not the vertical, compartmental one between denominations; it is the horizontal one, across all denominational lines, between liberals and conservatives. The actual cleavage, not ecclesiastical but of personal temperament, is between restive modernists and stiffening fundamentalists. The danger is that the increasing discomfort of the modernists who "interpret" their creeds and covenants out of their literal meaning will increasingly influence the defenders of the letter of the law to rigor and that the religiously easygoing middle-of-the-road folk, in their fright at the fury of the contemporary world, will retreat to this shelter of authority. In fact, we are witnessing an alarming rise in sectarian strictness and defensiveness among the champions of the "old-time religion." Parallel to the Roman Catholic banning of modernism and any flirtation with modern philosophies, fundamentalists, Anglo-Catholics, and conservatives join the swelling chorus which chants "As it was in our beginnings is now and ever shall be; world without end. Amen." Despite the alliance between liberals across sectarian boundaries, the Church seems to be anchored too fixedly to its past; and by its fixity more and more people are alienated. Orthodox churches boast of their remarkable growth, but how much of this influx is due to escapism from the duty of autonomous thinking? The proportion of nominal members is not ascertainable, but the national percentage of merely the non-affiliated populace is unmistakable evidence of their scorn or indifference to the appeal of orthodoxy.

Lest good-natured latitudinarians should be either forgetful of their own communions' cornerstone statements or unaware of their confreres' in other denominations, here are two or three examples of sectarian statements, each for a single communion.

Methodists have their Book of Discipline. Their standards of belief are based on Wesley's *Notes on the New Testament,* his *Five Articles,* and his sermons. Would our modern Methodists be quite comfortable with the evangelical naivete of "a free, full and present Salvation to every sinner—all men share in total depravity through the fall of Adam, a Salvation based on the Sacrifice of the Cross bestowed on condition of repentance toward God and faith toward our Lord Jesus Christ and certified inwardly by the witness of the Spirit of God and outwardly by a life of holy obedience"? To be sure, this is more mellow than some other denominational confessions, but "universal redemption" and "entire satisfaction" by the Sacrifice of the Cross still show a magical pattern.

Presbyterians are notably uncomfortable about their doctrine of predestination and election. Calvin's *Institutes* and the Westminster Confession may be their official platform, but Presbyterians consider it indelicate to quote them in full. "God from all eternity did, by the most wise and Holy Council of His Own will, freely and unchangeably ordain what soever comes to pass, yet so as thereby neither (sic) is God the author of sin or is violence offered to the will of His creatures. . . . Some men and angels are predestinated out of God's free grace and love, without any foresight of faith or good works, unto everlasting life; whose number is certain and definite, whereas the rest of mankind are foreordained to pass into everlasting death for their sin, to the praise of God's glorious justice." The grim logic of Adam's fall, of man's inherited and accumulated guilt, of the consequent justice of punishment and the limited number "effectually called" and adopted by God's absolute foreordaining "in spite of their sin and not of their merit" to the salvation which other luckless human beings doomed to eternal damnation can never have, no matter how hard they try to be righteous—all this is archaic *but creedal* for Calvin's church.

Baptist policy, like Congregationalist, is of parochial independence. Yet never may a Baptist church pass quite out of basic tradition. For instance, the *Northern Baptist Year Book* (1946-1949) has its statement, "Resolved, that we affirm our faith in the New Testament as a divinely inspired record and therefore a trustworthy, authoritative and all-sufficient rule of our faith and practice. We rededicate ourselves to Jesus Christ as Lord and Saviour and call our entire denomination to the common task of sharing the Whole Gospel with the whole world." The implications behind this, of revelation and atonement, are plain. Congregationalism, although more elastic, is on the same lines.

Lutheranism agrees on the Augsburg Confession as its common denominator. The twenty-one articles were bravely defiant of Rome's abuses and in their day they marked a tremendous advance; yet the preservation of their phrasing as conclusive for all time shows creedal idolatry. "Since Adam's fall, all men begotten after the common course of nature are born with sin; that is, without fear of God, without trust in Him and with fleshly appetite, and this disease or original fault is truly sin, condemning and bringing eternal death now also upon all that are not born again by baptism and the Holy Spirit." But by baptism "our sins are forgiven for Christ's sake, who by His death hath satisfied for our sins. This faith doth God impute for righteousness before Him."

The Thirty-Nine Articles of the Anglican communion are not the official statement of its present faith in America.

In England they still must be signed, as also the Athanasian Creed must be said on its minimum number of days. But in America they are printed at the back of the Prayer Book with a separate title page. Although thus technically outside the Prayer Book proper, there they abide, and woe to the man who rashly attempts to submit a resolution in Convention to remove them. These are their main items: "of Faith in the Holy Trinity," "three Persons, of one substance, power and eternity" (Article I); "of the Word or Son of God, which was made very Man, . . . begotten from everlasting of the Father, the very and eternal God and of one substance with the Father, took man's nature in the womb of the blessed Virgin" (Article II); of the "Resurrection of Christ . . . Who after death took again His Body, with flesh, bones and all things appertaining to the perfection of Man's nature; wherewith He ascended into Heaven and there sitteth until He return to judge all men at the last day" (Article IV). The Articles also affirm original sin, the denial of free will, salvation only by the name of Christ, and so on. All the key Articles are liturgically paraphrased in the Prayer Book itself, which throughout its sonorous and rhythmical cadences presents the identical dogmas. Every prayer but one ends with "through Jesus Christ our Lord" or the equivalent. Baptism is necessary since "none can enter into the kingdom of God except he be regenerate and born anew of water and the Holy Ghost"; the Holy Communion grants its participants "so to eat the flesh of Thy dear Son Jesus Christ and to drink His blood, that our sinful bodies may be made clean by His body and our souls washed through His most precious blood." In addition, the church is defined in the Nicene Creed as Catholic and *Apostolic,* and this is made more explicit in the Office of Institution where it is said that Jesus has "prom-

ised to be with the Ministers of Apostolic Succession to the
end of the world." What can liberal churchmen say in the
face of such unequivocal dicta?

No one can doubt the sincerity of convinced Anglo-Catholics, for in earnestness, devotion and consistency they average far more intensity than most easygoing liberals. Anglo-
Catholics, building on their initial cornerstone of magic grace,
give their creedal and ritual structure a logic which pre-
cludes all skepticism about its casuistry. They show a dedication which exasperates Protestants, but their system remains unscathed. They know they have authority.

As the Roman Church justifies its expanding development
on the authority of tradition as equal or superior to the mere
Biblical record ("The Church produced the New Testament,
not the New Testament the Church"), so the Anglo-Catholic
adapts the doctrine according to his own version of Catholic
tradition. Into the insufficient post-Resurrection story the
Catholic inserts his own conjecture and makes it his certitude,
to vindicate Apostolic Succession and its grace. As one ardent
proponent (and he a university professor of philosophy)
stated in my presence:

"In His forty days before the Ascension, our Blessed Lord
drew the blueprints for the Church which He committed
to the Apostles and their tactual successors, the Bishops, and
no one has the right to question those blueprints of the exclusive validity of the Episcopate, for to question them is to be
as traitorous as Judas Iscariot." If one could be inclined to
be humorous about so stern a pronouncement, he might picture the process of the chain of consecration which conveys
saving grace through the centuries almost as in rural days
water buckets were passed hand to hand up the line of fire

fighters from a pond to a conflagration. But one may not be facetious; the matter is too grave.

If the Episcopal Church could sever the shackles of outworn Christology and ecclesiology, if it could welcome scientific fact into its doctrines, expunge from its matchlessly phrased Prayer Book all its archaic terms, yet keep its liturgic dignity, beauty, and the aura of organic evolution from the past, it might sift and conserve the legitimate glories of its religious culture and face front with clean-cut modernity; it could then be the "bridge church" it likes to call itself instead of a drawbridge church with the draw span rusted up. It could combine the spaciousness of noble worship with a proper mysticism and a factual view of human life in one synthesis of corporate inspiration. It would not be handicapped by effete sacramentalism and outworn dogma. It could then rightly affirm its inclusiveness, its reverence before mystery, its social passion, and its proven membership with other communions in the body of a vital Christ on earth, *his* kind of Church. But as yet magic waters its ideas, ideals, ritual and attitudes.

Conventional Protestantism is still shackled by obsolete concepts—concepts of salvational magic.

What, therefore, are the possibilities of Church unity?

Church unity is a project in the hearts of all the sensitive liberals in the churches. Probably there is more of a guilt complex among them over the sin of the divided Church than over any other aspect of its life. To sectarianism must be ascribed the weakness of the Church's influence on world affairs. With shame for its ineffectiveness in any noble, inspiring, ethical way on governmental morals and morale, social conventions, on economics, civil rights, race relations, the use of the atom bomb, the whole crisis of peace versus war, the advocates of Church unity are sick at heart. "Onward Christian Soldiers" chokes in their throats, for it is nothing less than an inflated hypocrisy under the conditions of sectarian bigotry to sing:

> We are not divided;
> All one body we;
> One in faith and doctrine,
> One in charity.

All the arguments which demonstrate the iniquity of competitive sectarianism are patently true. Of course it is economically wasteful. Of course it bleeds small communities and advantageous city areas by insistence on the "true faith's" toehold. Of course its insulated and duplicated concerns deflect resources from vitally constructive programs into side issues. Of course its snobbishness negates charity, magnanimity, and contribution to the total cause. But all the arguments fail to change the sectarian psychosis. All the manifest reasons for unity are still up against such inbred unreasonableness as that of a local Jehu who was driving the author "down the island" when they passed two identical churches standing in the same yard—identical except for the steeple of one on the left and the other on the right. Jehu answered the natural query, saying, "Both of them's the same kind, only one's *hard* and the other's *free*. I really don't know the difference between 'em. I belong to the *free* one. I only know the other's a bunch of skunks."

The man on the sidewalk outside the church doors is puzzled at separatist quibblings. The phrases of the various covenants are filled with an incomprehensible vocabulary which common sense finds absurd. While World War III looms—which would end civilization in one hideous

Armageddon—he is aghast that Christians cannot be Christian. Why cannot they practice the brotherhood they preach? How can they read as Holy Writ Paul's chapters on spiritual authority?[1]

> For I say to every man among you, not to think of himself more highly than he ought to think, but to think soberly, according as God hath dealt to every man the measure of faith. . . .
> Now there are diversities of gifts, but the same Spirit. And there are differences of administration but the same Lord. And there are diversities of operation, but it is the same God that worketh all in all.

There are three theories of hypothetical oneness for the churches—union, uniformity, and unity. The words are not synonyms. *Union* is the organic oneness of a merged, centrally administered Church. *Uniformity* is the extension of the sectarian thesis, which would regularize and make unanimous the faith and liturgical form of that one Church. *Unity* allows elasticity in the practical co-operative activities but does not go beyond the broadest generalities of the common faith as the requisite for inclusion in the shared practicalities. Church union is improbable, if not impossible; Church uniformity is unthinkable and undesirable; Church unity is making great gains but its constituency is still required to be orthodox.

In all these three hypotheses the Roman Church is outside the scope. As has been sufficiently shown, it unalterably asserts that it is the only divinely commissioned Church and that all other communions are not valid. Therefore if there were to be union between Protestant, Eastern Orthodox, and Roman Catholic, it must be by complete surrender to the Roman doctrine and discipline. The prodigals must return in contrition; there can be no concessions to their heretical

---

[1] Romans 12; Corinthians 12.

convictions. Uniformity would then be automatic, for the Roman Catholic pattern would be the only one. As for Church unity, the Catholic Church can have no dealings or co-operative give and take for the sake of comity and joint enterprise, since its initial condition is submission to the papacy and to Catholic dogma.

But Church union is also incompatible with Protestant denominationalism, except in communions which differ from each other so little that economy, efficiency, and consanguinity are compelling obvious advantages. The cleavage between North and South which sundered most Protestantism at the time of the Civil War has so little to justify its perpetuation that reunion is overdue now that sectional disassociation has ceased to have any relevance. The only real obstacles, surmounted in some happy instances, have been the vested interests, officials who desired to keep their positions and, most of all, a contented laity more interested in undisturbed local parishes than in any Church-wide statesmanship.

The wartime schism has been healed in the Methodist and Presbyterian churches, North and South, and the same step is impending among liberal Baptist churches. The Congregational churches have merged with the "Christian" churches, and the Evangelicals with the Reformed in the Evangelical United Brethren Church. Several of the Lutheran Synods have merged. Language differences have become obsolete as second and third generations find no barriers in America between their original North European folk cultures. The independent Lutheran Synods have been more in number than their cousin communions under other inclusive names. Now, however, of the United Lutheran Church in America and thirty-two constituent Synods of the American Lutheran Conference, five have pooled their activities under the National Lutheran Council. And there have been two other minor mergers. With their basis of identical doctrine they could well do so. Yet the Synodical Conference, which includes in fundamentalist fellowship the powerful Missouri Synod and the Joint Synod of Wisconsin, will not budge from its intransigence for fear that the infiltration of liberalism in the National Lutheran Council will contaminate its own literalism.

The quarter-century record of the United Church of Canada has not yet been an example to be followed through in the United States by its larger Methodist, Presbyterian, and Congregational kindred. The organic union of those denominational families in Canada was the first of its kind since the Reformation. Nevertheless, in that Dominion there are still independent communions which have not responded to the invitation to union—the British Methodist Episcopal Church and the Church of England in Canada. Although one says "of course," the fault is not in the latter case with the Canadian Anglicans. Their negotiations on "a mutually acceptable ministry" were not met by any encouragement from the Lambeth Council in 1948, which was likewise embarrassed by the famous South India union in which the Indian Anglicans had gone their own enthusiastic way, to the mother church's perturbation.

All across the Protestant world liberal members chafe at the literalism of their own brethren. But they are hoist by their own sectarian petard. Although they feel an obligation to defend fewer dogmas with any rigidity, they are withheld from bold venture for union by the threats of secession by the "true believers," and they hesitate to precipitate further splits in the Church.

As a conspicuous example of the sovereignty complex, the

Anglo-Catholic wing of the Protestant Episcopal Church and the Church of England affirms its veto right against any union which does not begin with the acknowledgment that the authority and commission of the Church is in the Historic Episcopate and that any church which fails to accept this and its corollary theory of the valid sacraments and grace is not a church at all. This nearly approximates the Roman Catholic criterion. In fact, the Anglo-Catholic bloc repudiates the Protestant classification of the Episcopal communion and would even change its name to Catholic if it could. The Reformation may have set all the churches free from papal rule, but for the Anglo-Catholic there is no discomfort with Catholic doctrine.[2]

In a burst of enthusiasm by a liberal majority, the General Convention of the Protestant Episcopal Church once enacted a resolution to seek organic union with the Presbyterian Church, U. S. A. The gusto waned as the High Church minority lifted its voice to quote the established formulae of

[2]There is perhaps no greater incongruity in all church life than the existence of Anglo-Catholicism inside the communion still officially named the Protestant Episcopal. For illustration, see the following quotations from a "Catechism of Worship" issued by the Society of St. John the Evangelist (the "Cowley Fathers") of that church:

"How do we use holy water?"
We dip our fingers in the water and cross ourselves.
"What help shall we get from using holy water?"
We shall be helped against evil spirits, because they hate the symbol of purity and flee from it.
"What is the Lord's Service?"
The Lord's Service is the holy eucharist, commonly called mass.
"What happens when the priest repeats our Lord's words: 'This is my body,' 'This is my blood'?"
When the priest repeats our Lord's words, the bread and wine become the body and blood of our Lord.
"How can God make bread and wine become His body and blood?"
God can make bread and wine become body and blood because He is Almighty.
"How do I know that He makes the bread and wine His body and blood?"
Because He said so.
(The doctrine of the Real Presence teaches us that, just as during His life on

the exclusive potence possessed only by communions with Apostolic orders. The Commission on Approaches to Unity debated at length whether the Presbyterian Church *is* a church with which the Episcopal Church could treat on any basis of equality, and the eventual vote was that the Presbyterian Church *is* a church according to its *own* definition of what a church is! And, at a later joint meeting with the Presbyterian Commission, an Anglo-Catholic bishop said with a sweet smile to the moderator of the Presbyterian Assembly, "But you know, you have no grace!" "Have we any goodness? If so, where do we get it?" queried the moderator. To which there could be no pertinent answer. The proposal of the merger is now a dead issue on both sides; for the meaningless subsequent resolution of the General Conventions merely submits it as "worthy of serious study." But the High Church minority will still argue that the proposed merger "radically distorts the religion of Our Lord and is repugnant to the mind of Christ!"

If union is impossible, except in minor ways, uniformity is more impossible, and for the added reason that uniformity should never have been an ideal anyway. It would lockstep spontaneity under the eye of authoritarian guards. Much of the apathy or antagonism to Church unity comes from the complete misunderstanding of its objective as being uniformity. The absolutism which could enforce robot unanimity

---

earth the Divine Spirit of our Blessed Lord dwelt in a material human body, so now, by the action of the Holy Ghost, He is truly and entirely present in the consecrated bread and wine of the Blessed Sacrament.)

"Why do we keep the Feast of the Assumption of the Virgin?"

We keep the Feast of the Assumption in remembrance of the Blessed Virgin's being received into glory [August 16].

"Why do we believe in the Assumption?"

We believe in the Assumption because the Saints of God are all in Heaven and the Blessed Virgin is Queen of all the Saints.

would sacrifice every freedom personality deserves and must have.

Church unity—to do what can be done—increasingly bypasses separatist dogma and attempts a co-operative, loose confederation merely in the practicalities. Local councils of churches, state councils, now the National Council of the Churches of Christ in America, and the World Council of Churches all go forward on a teamwork plan. But the teamwork of this National Council and World Council is limited to the denominations which are specifically grounded in their faith "in Jesus Christ as God and Savior." Even so, an antagonistic federation of fundamentalists, the American Council of Churches, stays out, in opposition to the "liberalism" of the National Council, while the Unitarians, Universalists, Humanists, Ethical Culturists, and the Friends are excluded from participation because they cannot hold to the authoritarian qualifications of magicized "Christianity."

In November 1950, the National Council of the Churches of Christ in America was inaugurated on the greatest scale of co-operation the Western world has known. It is no "super-church"; it is not an organic union. Its preamble says:

In the Providence of God the time has come when it seems fitting more fully to manifest the essential oneness of the Christian Churches of the United States of America in Jesus Christ as their divine Lord and Savior by the creation of an inclusive co-operative agency.

It was a momentous time for the included denominations when their leaders, clad in the gowns or vestments of their rites, joined the great procession to the signatory table and each denomination's representative stepped forward and signed the constituting document, to be followed by the representatives of the eight[3] interchurch administrative organizations which had hitherto worked separately. Twenty-five Protestant and four Eastern Orthodox denominations,[4] the Federal Council of the Churches of Christ in America, the Foreign Missions Conference, the International Council of Religious Education, the Home Missions Council, the Missionary Education Movement, the National Protestant Council on Higher Education, the United Council of Church Women, and the United Stewardship Council—all these are in the roster. The step taken by the participant groups is a tremendous one for them, for two-thirds of the American communions and their thirty-one million communicants are theoretically involved. But the propagandist proclamation that this established an "Ecumenical Church" is beyond truth; for that is exactly what the National Council *is not*. For illustration, there could have been no great Communion Service at the meeting. Imagine the explosion which would have been touched off by any suggestion of one! All the issues of orders and grace would have intruded at once and the plan would have been wrecked.

The World Council of Churches may set up Interchurch Life and Work or Faith and Order Conferences; the National Council may include among its directives the encouragement of "devotional fellowship and mutual counsel"—but there is no evading the fundamental fact that co-operation without union is not the "essential oneness of the Christian Churches." The Amsterdam Conference of the World Conference, for instance, was not even able to agree on a definition of "Church," although the Edinborough Conference had made it plain that among the denominations there is no cleavage on basic doctrine, only of polity. Neverthe-

---

[3]Four more have since joined.
[4]The Greek Orthodox Church also joined in 1952.

less, the ideal of practical co-operation proves at least that liberal-minded Christians, getting their inspiration inside their own churches, have come to the conviction that faith can show itself in works and that true Christianity begins at the church door going *out* into the world of need where they join shoulder to shoulder with others who have learned their duty in other churches. Ministrations of real good, which would go halting under insulated auspices, become feasible. Teachers can be taught their techniques in expert training schools; religious surveys can be made and placement of new churches arrived at in comity. A legislative lobby can be conducted for general religious interests. Motion pictures can be produced jointly and white lists of the commercial output circulated. Skilled religious drama can be given wider use. Religious book weeks can be sponsored. Summer schools can be conducted. Social service can be effectively furthered. By working together, churchfolk should learn how little their sectarian dogmas and rituals really count in comparison with that which applied good can accomplish in the world.

What a pity it is that this trend remains so gravely handicapped by obstinate obstructionists who lift the cry of their own bigotry against the many who do not accept their particular definition of Christianity. One is tempted to quote Job's sarcastic words to his "comforters": "No doubt ye are the people and wisdom shall die with you." Would not the harrowed face of the Son of Man gaze in amazement at those who, in His name, pretend to private information about the "mind of God." Would not he exclaim, "Ye fools and blind, why beholdest thou the mote that is in thy brother's eye but considerest not the beam that is in thine own eye? Ye hypocrites, how is it ye do not discern the times?" Fundamentalism, in all its varieties, degrees, passions, and obscurantisms, is fundamentally opposed to the liberalism of Jesus.

All honor to the progressive churchmen and churchwomen who have at all dared to circumvent creedal opinionativeness and inaugurate co-operative practicalities. The proponents of these activities are in the van of Protestantism. Nevertheless, on the other hand it must be pointed out that in carrying through these very co-operative projects, Liberals have delivered themselves into the hands of the reactionary members of their denominations who have set their fundamentalist standards as obligatory.

This limited co-operation among the first-cousin Protestant-isms does not justify really ecumenical claims. What has been accomplished is an obdurate denominational separatism on a new scale. To exclude all who cannot subscribe to a belief "in Jesus Christ as God and Savior," even if they are Christian in their wholehearted faith in the religion Jesus had, is only to enlarge and ratify and make final the sectarian mistake.

CHAPTER SIX

Christian Science

In recent times no new denomination has been founded on so daring a thesis, has caused so much controversy, has spread so fast and so far, and has won so permanent a place in the roster of religions as has Christian Science. Almost in our own generation, it has passed from its first stage when it was accused of mawkish quackery, through its second stage when it was called by the more dignifying name of a heresy, into the third and present stage when it must be accepted as one of the denominations, a church among the churches.

Of course there are fiery opponents who still think it is sheer quackery; and there are those who still contemptuously argue what seem to them its arrant heresies, its scientific absurdity, its bureaucracy, and its idolatry of Mother Eddy's life and message. Nevertheless, the Christian Science Church has now won established prestige. Why? Because, despite the fact that Christian Science will not cure the ills of many of its members, Christian Science has met an otherwise unmet longing.

It could never have come to such established strength if it had *not* provided something which other religions did not appear to offer. Its success indicates how little we average human beings live by inelastic and adamantine logic based on extrinsic fact, and how much we all live by wish-thinking rationalizations and emotional drives. Even though Christian Science's enemies claim that its results are gained—if gained they are—by fictitious and unsound means, yet, for most of us, humane ends may justify strange means. For the great number of adherents for whom Christian Science physically and spiritually avails, nothing succeeds like success. For the unconfessed number of those who have tried it and found their last state worse than their first, nothing fails like failure. Yet as the Pope said of Francis of Assisi and his quite different venture, "If to accept the plain words of the Gospel is heresy, that would be a strange mystery."

Mrs. Eddy found her thesis in selected passages of Jesus' healings and preaching. She is not to be blamed by competitors whose glass houses of literalism have stood longer unstoned. But what denominationalist hasn't his own collection of proof texts picked according to *his* theory?

Without dissecting the stark dogmas of Christian Science in detail, the generalization appears to be fair that in their first stage, they were bizarre and crude. Mrs. Eddy's adoption of Mr. Quimby's mind-over-matter mottoes and practices was her suggesting impetus. Daringly and consistently she went on from them. Her Divine Metaphysics had its initial occasion in her own healing in 1866. That date is to be noted, for in that period there were rampant fundamentalisms of great variety and vapidity. Discipline over religious intemperateness was feeble. It is to Mrs. Eddy's credit that at first she intended no separate church; for she sincerely—if naively—hoped that her discovery would be taken up by all denominations. She believed it was a legitimate deduction from their shared evangel. She said, "I knew the principle of all-harmonious Mind-Action to be God, and that cures were produced in primitive Christianity by holy, uplifting faith. . . . and I won my way to absolute conclusions through divine revelation, reason and demonstration."

Perhaps if the churches had been more open to her idea, it might have helped them as well as kept the theory of Christian Science from becoming extreme. But, as with all heresies since established religions began, the repudiation of their heretical doctrines compelled proponents of the "new truth" to extravagances to which they otherwise might not have gone. The doctrine that "God is Love and there is no such reality as pain or evil" evolved into hypnotic magic and evoked results which made the Wednesday evening testimonial meetings prosper.

Christian Science did not and does not make any diagnostic distinction between organic and functional ills. When the ailment is functional, i. e., nervously centered, any integrating and affirmative autosuggestion, working strongly on one's inmost life, is likely to have derivative results and often shows amazing cures. Even in some organic troubles such as tuberculosis, autosuggestion or vital faith has alleviative effectiveness. But when an organic malady is as definite as cancer or diphtheria, the suggestion that all evil is only an error of mortal mind does not take the place of a physician. (Mrs. Eddy herself went to the dentist.) Many are the hushed-up tragedies which need not have happened if the distinction between functional and organic illness had not been ignored in Christian Science. There is noble truth behind the creed that God is the only Might or Mind and that all Reality is in the God who is Love.

But in Science's day-by-day usages, thaumaturgy creeps into the incantation of catchwords, and into the elevation of *Science and Health* to co-equality with the Bible in public services and in personal demonstrations. The authoritarian power of the Mother Church organization is absolute. The reverent trust shown by applicants for absent treatment by healers is as implicit as a communicant's for his priest's intercessions.

If today's Christian Scientists dared to be radically confidential, they would admit that Mrs. Eddy's passing somewhat permitted a new movement of adaptation to the modern mood. In fact, back in 1910, a leading Scientist secretly suggested to this author that Science had prepared for her death with some new adaptation to freer policies.

There has also been a quiet expurgation of bothersome extravagances such as the veiled prophecy, in the enthusiastic first edition of the manual of faith, that births will be virginal like Jesus' if we truly "demonstrate" the truth. The crass accusation of malicious animal magnetism has been less and less heard. Under certain conditions non-medicinal treatments by osteopaths, chiropractors, and doctors have been permitted. A ruthless censorship has well-nigh obliterated all the less than ideal facts of Mrs. Eddy's adaptation of Mr. Quimby's panaceas of theory and treatment, of her own successive marriages, and of her arbitrary dictation of her church polity for all time. Georgette Milmine's documented biography has been completely suppressed.

There has been something of a change for the better in Christian Science. It has begun a liberalization and modernization of its dogmatic literalism and has ceased being merely so exaggeratedly a non-medicinal medicine to cure ills and pains. It has endeavored to voice a more spiritual religiousness more worthy of classification as a church. The Divine Principle has made Science a faith for more cultural purposes and philosophic idealism than at the outset. Although of necessity it retains its Founding Mother's sacrosanct *Key to the Scriptures,* it makes tentative use of psychology and psychiatric techniques.

The publications of Christian Science rank among the topmost of our nation. The *Quarterly* and *Journal* and *Sentinel* have been domestic, of course, but the *Monitor* performs a superb public service as possibly the best daily newspaper in America—unbiased, unhysteric, internationally informed, giving no indecent parade of crime, sifting out truly important news with consistent poise and clarity and with no blatant propagation of Christian Science as such even in the fine editorials which bring spiritual standards into public and personal life.

Nevertheless, the modification of policy and polity and its free evolution out of magic into rationality are definitely limited. Will it always be? Will its lecturers ever submit their authorized explanations to factual debate? Will the presentations of Christian Science expand beyond the limits of Mrs. Eddy's inflexible formulae?

Christian Science is for those who can "swallow faggots crosswise" under the spell of a noble half-truth. The picture of Christian Science's own Mother Mary smiles down sweetly and assuringly on the earnest, half-magic-half-mystic church which she bequeathed to the world. Will it remain true to its faith according to her sacred *Key to the Scriptures*? Or will its rationale develop more in consonance with reason and science?

CHAPTER SEVEN

Credulities

Beyond the spectrum of the usual constituted churches, there is the ultraviolet of esoteric religions and cults and the infrared of outright superstition. Although there are some common characteristics, the two are separable. Yet the esoteric religions and cults, however naive, are at least coherent groups, while superstitions are individual and incoherent. The followers of this or that Pied Piper make up only minority groups. They have little social impact. And, although superstitions are amazingly prevalent, they play only a minor part in the total social psychology. As a whole, they reveal a subconscious immaturity and mental pathology which is deep-seated. The name of peripheral religions is legion. Among the hundreds, we will mention only those which are better known. Yet see how the virus of magic works in them all.

NAIVE RELIGIONS

It should be self-evident that no heterodox faith gathers to itself a starry-eyed membership unless somewhere in its doctrine there is something which promises the fulfillment of some longing which is indelible in human nature, the answer to some hunger that the established churches have not quite fed.

Reversing the trend which has made the major religions less noble than their founders, many of these abnormal fellowships have improved upon their founders, especially when those founders formulated their revelations in a cruder era. Yet, in such cases, there may also have been a semi-deification of that founder which, to the followers, makes his or her prestige invulnerable to damaging facts.

1. *MRA and the Oxford Group*

The Reverend Frank Buchman began his movement on the basis of "changed" individuals, one by one. His "Absolutes" were four: Absolute Honesty, Absolute Purity, Absolute Unselfishness, and Absolute Love. He was a one-man revivalist team, with an uninhibited audacity for dragging sins out into the light. He insisted on the "morning watch" and inner quiet, in order to get "guidance" for the day. "Guidance" was to be waited for in the tiniest details of life; the Holy Spirit would speak directions for every moment's actions. Those who had "come clean" were to go out and win souls by demanding the same "change" in others. He standardized the five "C's": Confidence, Confession, Conviction, Conversion, and Continuance. He emphasized sex sins with an almost Freudian passion. He had hypnotic power over innerly uncomfortable people. He dared to pry open the conventional lives of complete strangers and haul out their secrets. He did not wait for them to divulge their sins; he had uncanny intuitions and flatly accused them.

In the colleges of Oxford he organized his converts into a "First Century Fellowship" or Oxford Group. Then he came to America. The technique he had perfected was appropriate for our universities and then beyond them. He organized house parties in the most gracious homes or inns he could find, where the Quiet Time and public confessions, called "sharing," were pressed, and the technique taught to new converts. The group tended to the "up-and-inners" rather than the "down-and-outers" and many a social or political leader found an unexpected tang in the experience of "Guidance." Money flowed in. Expense was no deterrent to any "Guided" project, journey, or overhead.

Then Buchman's humility, never great, disappeared in a complex of near Messianic vision. He dreamed of the metamorphosis of the nations into one great Oxford Group. Back in England, there was no stopping his attack on key people. He believed in audacity. Leaders were his quarry. From England he moved over to the Continent and crashed the gates of statesmen, tycoons, admirals, and generals. He began to talk of Moral Re-armament as the salvation of governments and peoples. And he had such success that he considered himself the builder of the bridge between the nations and the agent of the Kingdom of God in practical affairs. He saw Chamberlain off for Munich and welcomed him home. He publicly thanked God for Hitler and Mussolini and other dictators who, if they could be converted, would bring whole nations to "the Jesus Way." He told the League of Nations Assembly, "The Voice of God through you will become the will of the people." He cried that "the Day of Miracles is not over." He telephoned from London to a big American gathering, "America must re-arm spiritually or all is lost." The individuated Oxford Group methods were now superseded by the world-changing hope. From Madison Square Garden to the Hollywood Bowl he and his cohorts progressed, arriving on the West Coast in a twenty-two car special train. The list of testifying converts read like pages from *Who's Who*. At the Del Monte World Assembly for Moral Re-armament he read good will messages from King George VI and Queen Elizabeth, from premiers of every nation where MRA had campaigned, from forty-two governors, and from President Roosevelt. ("The underlying strength of the world must consist in the moral fibre of her citizens." Who wouldn't subscribe to that abstract principle?) "New men, new nations, a new world"; "MRA is the essential foundation for world settlement"; "Where God guides, God provides"! So said Buchman.

But when the war came, the flamboyant confidence of MRA faded away; there were defections by the thousand. The "preview of a new world order" was not made good. Buchman's pre-war statements boomeranged; for example, "Systems don't matter, whether capitalism, Fascism, Communism. The worst system will work if God guides it." Buchman was *persona non grata* overseas. The movement faltered. His New York headquarters at Calvary Church were taken away from him. He moved headquarters to Mackinac Island. Buchman today is not well. The world has failed him. Only the die-hard loyalists keep on. The magic did not work.

2. *Eastern Derivatives*

The miscellaneous corner of each Saturday's church advertisements in the newspapers presents a menu of strange isms. Among them are sundry oriental fellowships which range in dignity from Bahai and Vedanta down through Theosophy and New Thought to Rosicrucianism and Maz-daz-lan, Homes of Truth and Hotel Parlor Healers. For their own sake one could wish for such swamis as Vivekananda and his confreres a better classification than the usual listing provides. For they preach a true Yoga which is mystically disciplinary and psychologically spiritual. They themselves must shrink from being lumped in with the mountebanks who boast that they "spray the mind with psychic energy, unlock personal magnetism, guarantee the destruction of malicious cosmic influences, bring Supernal Fulfillment to desires for Love, Business Success, and Inviolable Vigor of Health" by a ten-dollar course of lessons with all the Yoga clichés.

Bahai has a superb ideal. Stemming from the Persian prophet Bahā'u'llāh ("the splendor of God"), Bahai has a Messianic expectation of its Utopia-to-be when all nations and religions will bury their differences and merge their truths. Bahā'u'llāh said that the spokesmen of the world's faiths were each a mirror of the glory of God, equal in worth. Persecuted and harried in the East, the Bahaists (disciples) eventually were carried to the prison city of Akka, where Bahā'u'llāh was hideously maltreated and imprisoned, until his awesome saintliness forced a less horrible incarceration. His sufferings bred a deification by the time of his death in 1892.

His son Abdul-Bahā inherited imprisonment for forty years. At last, when the Turkish revolution set him free, he set out to find a spot where good will reigned, and finally came to America. His missionary travels across our country were a seven-day sensation to the uncomprehending public. Delirious believers were extravagant in their emotional abandon. His mystical Ideal was that all people will be manifestations of the love of Bahā'u'llāh; that each one may "become like a clear lamp of crystal from which the rays of the bounties of the Blessed Perfection may shine forth to all nations and peoples." At Willmette, Illinois, the cathedral of the faith has been erected, and local Spiritual Assemblies here and there across the land look to the national one. The more than three thousand members of the movement are sure that someday not too far in the future the United Nations will be transcended by an International House of Justice stressing the Oneness of Mankind.

This lofty dream is handicapped by a tendency to numerology and the tradition of embodied mystical authority descending from the Bak to Bahā'u'llāh to Abdul-Bahā and now to Shoghi Effendi, the grandson. The habits of oriental speech make the Bahai scripture seem too purple for Western consumption. There is an aura of esoteric unrealism which simply does not impress hard-headed realists. To them there is a suggestion of a too cloying sweetness.

Is there any need to dwell on New Thought, Theosophy, Rosicrucianism, and such? These are the sources of most of the more raw, cabalistic hocus-pocus which staggers common sense by its delusions of grandeur. Since the Purple Mother, Katherine Tingley, set up the Point Loma Theosophical Society and her Raja Yoga College a half-century ago, to be followed by Madam Blavatsky; and since Annie Besant produced the New Messiah, Krishnamurtri, enthroned in the Ojai Valley, Theosophy has spread its spell. The secret doctrine of the Brotherhood of Adepts or Mahatmas in Tibet, who have made the body "the ductile instrument of Intelligence," has thousands of illumined pupils who embrace Brahman explanations of human happiness or misery as the process of Karma, the working out of our previous incarnations' due reward or punishment. Would that theosophy could shed its extremisms and be a plain theory.

New Thought is actually old thinking, exaggerated with melodramatic flourishes by amateurs at Hindu philosophy. In the procession of faked orientalisms come the Great White Brotherhoods, the Mystical Order of Melchizedek, the Shangri-La Nudist Camps which camouflage their sexual allure by a bit of Zoroastrian sun worship, the Maz-daz-lans who attain salvation by rythmic breathing, and the "I AM'S" who provide "the Ascended Master's Gift of Wealth, Energy and the Cup of Pure Electronic Essence through the Atomic Accelerator, with all the power of the I AM who spoke from the Burning Bush and in the seven I AM'S from the lips of Jesus, the Word-Made-Flesh". . . .

Gullibility is a religious phenomenon we cannot laugh off. Exposure of fraud does not convince men who think they need magic to make their lives bearable.

3. *The Mormons*

There could be no more apt an example of the improvement of faith over its first days than that of Mormonism. The incongruity of the shady tale of its founder, Joseph Smith, with the present substantial and impressive estate of the Church of Jesus Christ of Latter Day Saints is almost incredible. The story of the Golden Plates which were "translated" into the Book of Mormon is preposterous. But it was the foundation of the heroism of the pioneers and stability of the present church. In its practices Mormonism is no crackpot cult. Mormonism has triumphantly weathered storms of persecution and ridicule. Its fundamantal tenets have been easily proven fantastic. Its versions of God's dealings with his people on the Western Continent after the Tower of Babel overseas is not even good myth. There is not a vestige of evidence for any item of Smith's tale. His own character gives no shred of prestige for his pretentious claims. Yet, most individual Mormons are sturdy, sincere, honorable, and fine citizens.

The contemporary worth of the Latter Day Saints in our democracy makes most people under-emphasize their dogmas. But there they *are* in the Book of Mormon, the "Doctrine and Covenants" and that "Pearl of Great Price" in which Moses and Abraham gave to God's Prophet, Seer, and "Revelator" their infallible exposition of the Existence of Time, Matter, Space, the Universe, and the External Mind, and of the Kingdoms or World Systems inhabited by Intelligences in their various stages of development.

Crudity cannot be outgrown as long as this scripture is held as the divinely given supplement to the New Testament and of equal validity. However, the change in prestige from an earlier time to our own day can be illustrated by the change in temper between the 1884 edition of the *Britannica* and the most recent edition in its treatment of Mormonism. The summary of doctrine in the current article omits many of the damaging statements which the savage earlier treatment features. It now stresses that members have the right to divine guidance through revelation to individual lives "even superior to the written word." It stipulates that, although individual believers share with those of earlier times the privilege of continuous revelation by the visible Presence of God by the visitation of Angels, yet "impressions upon the mind by the Spirit of God" are *also* the means of truth.

Nevertheless the fundamental of all fundamentals is Joseph Smith's prophetic assertions. Even the gentler modern interpretation is obliged to retain the word "alleged" with regard to his "revelation." Do we know its story?

This son of "poor, ignorant, thriftless and not too honest parents" began to have his "alleged" visions when only fifteen. God the Father and Jesus Christ appeared to him in person to mark him out for their special purpose; then the angel Moroni appeared and told him that the Bible of the Western Continent was buried nearby. So in due time Smith followed directions and the angel delivered to him a stone box containing a volume of thin gold plates, the plates covered with small writing in the "reformed" Egyptian tongue, and also a pair of supernatural spectacles called the "Interpreters," the crystals of which were Urim and Thummim, by the aid of which the mystic characters could be read. Since Smith was illiterate he employed a man named Cowdery as his amanuensis "to whom, from behind a curtain he dictated a translation." And so on.

The preface to the Book of Mormon includes the testimonial of Cowdery and two others that they saw the plates. Cowdery and his companions later repudiated this testimony and denied they had ever seen the plates. The plates were never produced, " having been taken back by the angel after they had been translated." And the source of the Book has been found in a historical romance written in 1812 by one Solomon Spalding, a "crack-brained preacher," a copy of which was directly traced into Smith's hands.

The Mormon faith is Christ-centered and is therefore Trinitarian. But it has its extra doctrines such as that of unborn spirits craving birth that they may grow souls (which gave plural marriage its reason), of the sealing "for time and eternity" of earthly mates, of the Translated Beings for whom death is suspended, and of the reign of perfected saints over the inhabitants of planets and stars. Isn't this faith in magic?

4. *The Swedenborgians*

In 1744, Emanuel Swedenborg, the beloved, strange Assessor of the College of Mines at Upsala, turned from his curious mechanical and geometrical theory of the origin of things and became a supernaturalist and prophet. He said that heaven had been opened to his spiritual sight and that the Lord had manifested Himself in person. In his dreams and trances he had overheard mysterious conversations in the spiritual world and the Lord had filled him with His Spirit to teach the doctrine of the New Church by the word from Himself. He had been permitted to see the heavens and hells and to converse with angels and other spirits. But the doctrine came directly from the Lord alone.

This exhalted rhapsody consumed him. He gave up all worldly learning and devoted himself to exhaustive writings in Latin which developed his "Key of Correspondences" which unlocked the divine treasure of wisdom about the true states of men and women in the next life, the scenery and occupations of heaven and hell, the origin of evil, and the sanctity and perpetuity of marriage. But most startling of all, he asserted that the Last Judgment had already come to pass, in 1757, and that he had been a witness of that momentous event. And he, the Paraclete of the Last Dispensation, had been told to found the New Church or New Jerusalem for the saved souls the Lord had given him. The "Key of Correspondences" between the natural and the spiritual world had been given him, with which to unlock the divine treasures of wisdom. From God, the Divine Man, radiates a Divine Sphere, which is as the sun to the spiritual world, and from this sun the sun in the natural cosmos is derived, and man lives by both suns in both worlds.

Swedenborg's prolific writings had glimpses of fine ethics, profound glances of insight into the depths of human life, but the main body of his thought is so astoundingly deluded that it is hard to understand his following. *Arcana Coelestia* (in eight quarto volumes), *Apocalypsis Explicata,* and *Sapientia Angelica de Divine Amore et de Divina Sapientia* are the principal expositions of his revelation. They are characterized by extravagant anthropomorphism, mechanical materialism, theological narrowness, allegorizing, a total absence of historical knowledge and unbelievable prophecy—all available in their English translation, advertised for free distribution, under an evidently substantial endowment fund.

The Swedenborgian Church bases its authority on its founder's participation in that Last Judgment two centuries ago. The divine commission given him to expound the three-fold sense of the Word — natural, spiritual, and celestial — is continued for his church. Its members carry on in his spirit. They believe that heaven and hell are like the soul to the natural body, in and around our natural life, and that unconsciously, or, if we are spiritualized, consciously, we inhabit it. The end of creation is that man may become the image of his Creator. By Jesus Christ, the only God, in whom is the Trinity (the Father, His infinite divine nature; the Son, His glorified human nature and divine body; the Holy Spirit, the life from Him for our salvation), the believers assure themselves of their salvation.

Swedenborgians themselves tend to be gentle, poetic, evangelical, and appealing. But theirs is a doctrine of magic.

5. *Father Divine*

Joseph Smith and Emanuel Swedenborg were of the past. Father Divine is very much of the present.

He is ludicrous, yes — yet he is also humble, canny, humorous, and devoted. His is not a mere racket. To his lowly followers, black and white, now more than a million in number, he has been the inspiration to made-over lives. He "visibilates" and "tangibilates" God to them. His grandiloquent vocabulary may be outlandish but his disciplines are rigorous; "True God Father Divine" demands that his initiates clean up past sins, make restitution for them, pay off even forgotten debts, and live purely as in "the Spirit of the Consciousness of the Presence of God" which he radiates. The assertions of this "God in the Flesh" are a kind of double talk, for with constant finesse he phrases his many-syllabled proclamations so that if challenged (which he never is by his ecstatic adorers) he could carry the accusation of purely personal possession of divinity by saying it is the birthright of all. Yet he, "the Living Fundamental" — whose assumed name is the key to ex-George Baker's glorification — allows the inference of his personal "visibilation" of God to be only his own. "Peace! It's wonderful!" is incarnate in him.

It is easy to laugh at surface characteristics of this Peace Mission Movement and Father Divine's inflated pious jingoism. His converts choose new names which are more than eccentric — Live Dove, Virgin Rose, Bunchalove, Universal Cheerfulness, David Consolation, Rapid Integration, Pearly Gates — but they show the inhibited yearnings for significance. Father Divine is married, in a spiritual sense, to a white Sweet Angel called the Holy Virgin Mother. The Rosebuds or choirs lift spirituals into a new afflatus. The Holy Communion banquets at Heaven's Table run to scores of prodigal courses of free food. Peace Groceries, Peace Beauty Parlors, and Peace Laundries offer cut rates so far below normal that they are accounted miraculous. The spiritual co-operatives of the movement include the farms, hotels, stores, and vacation homes constantly being added to, particularly in greater New York and upstate, in Philadelphia, and in California. Father Divine's real estate holdings are worth more than $6,000,000. There are foreign groups in Canada, England, and Australia. The International Righteous Government Department unabashedly looks forward to the state of the world its name denotes. *The New Day* is its newspaper, with the dateline always marked ADFD — Anno Domini Father Divine!

The phenomenon of such a travesty on religion in this our day should give us pause. "True God Father Divine" is indeed far above voodoo and his influence on his tremendous flock is far beyond a racial one. Whatever his egregious near-blasphemy, his "visibilation" of God has "tangibilated" what so many people crave.

6. *And Others*

Once in a while a Jehovah's Witness on a street corner tries to sell us a copy of the *Watch Tower* which announces that the end of the age is near, that "Satan the Devil" has the churches in his grip, that "Jehovah God" commands that His faithful shall have no part in the quarrels of the children of men or the governments of the earth. Therefore it is a sin to salute the flag or to vote, because this would be a false worship. But are we aware of the scope of the Witnessing which is going on? IBSA, the Watch Tower Bible and Tract Society, has its own presses which print twenty thousand bound books and one hundred and fifty thousand booklets per *day*, twenty million per year. There are over seventy thousand distributors. There are Kingdom Halls in almost every urban center. Every Witness, obeying Isaiah ("Ye are my witnessess") and Paul ("Witness in every city"), goes doggedly from house to house to play the standard phonograph record of Armageddon's nearness, to sell the Theocracy's literature, to publish the Truth in person. And there is a market for these wares.

In the miasma of credulity thrive such sects as the snake-handling Holiness orgiasts, the Fire Baptized Holiness, the National David Spiritual Temple of Christ Church Union, Inc., the Church of the Living God the Pillar and Ground of Truth, the House of David, and others of least adult caliber. There are two hundred and thirty bodies in the almanac's list, of which anachronistic fellowships are by far the majority named. Outside the conventional but unrealist churches there is indeed a wide penumbra of medicine-man heterodoxy. Truly Religious maturity is as yet far from achieved by the mass mind.

Here is an instance: between the World Wars, a private society was formed "For Testing Human Credulity." It was called HIRAF, which is a manufactured name. Among its experiments was the preparation of a soulful paper as meaningless as four writers, working separately in jumbled, high-flown malapropisms, could contrive. Scrambled into one document and solemnly submitted, it was promptly accepted and published by the official organ of spiritualism. Madam Blavatsky praised it for its philosophical insight into hidden Truth, and Mrs. Besant quoted it as an authority on Theosophical doctrine. Its nonsense can be guessed by such sentences as these from the guileful article:

"In the name of Ra, Isis, Ainsoph and Eglobal: with the minor integers of the ALL, neither create nor uncreate can be predicted. Their experiences are from Chaos into their reassociation with the Divine—until, therefore, the solemn moment of apotheistic concomitance, the passage of the soul goes on. The microcosm is ONE in its end, viz, the attainment of the third physical emanation of the spiritual and the final co-association with the EU-SOPH."

SUPERSTITIONS

At the beginning of this chapter, superstitions were described as individual and incoherent. They are not the specific doctrine of any organized cult. They are instead the vagaries of irrational people who do not have a cogent theory for their furtive perpetuation.

Superstitions are vestigial survivals of aboriginal or pagan folk faith. Every one of them has some fetishist or shamanist ancestry. Almost unchanged from archaic usage, they recall the tom-toms and sorcery or the awed Mystery rituals which the Church of the Dark Ages incorporated. There is an inherited subconsciousness in man's genes which makes him attempt obscurely motivated would-be magic for which he can give no rational explanation.

Horoscopes have not changed their divinations since Babylonian Magi cast them by the rotation of the seven planets and the combinations of stars on birth dates. Their deductions were according to the Houses of the Zodiac, which were the ancients' astronomic maximum. All the development of scientific astronomy from Ptolemy to Mt. Palomar means nothing to today's buyers of horoscope magazines. Newspaper forecasts by the stars are a standard item. Countless devotees thumb their pulp Bibles of prophecy before investing money or venturing on any other personal project. Hitler is not the only fuehrer who planned campaigns by horoscopes. The card catalog of almost any big library lists astrology under science. The predictions are so generalized that addicts can find an occasional vindication by events, while they conveniently forget the usual times when nothing of the sort forecast under their planet for ten o'clock last Friday came to pass.

Numerology equals astrology in its sway and is often blended into it. The jugglery of rudimentary arithmetic repeats the awe for numbers felt by their earliest manipulators. Ignorant people were dazed by the behavior of perfect numbers and were repelled by the obstinacy of odd ones. Twelves and abacus combinations were eerie. Lucky versus unlucky numbers were ascribed to the powers of good fortune over against Satan's. So, today, the digits of our automobile number or the computation of values in the letters of a motion picture starlet's alias "guarantee" that the goblins won't get you, forsooth. Oh, perfect twelves — so divisible, so complete! Twelve tribes, twelve hours, twelve months, Twelfth Night, dozens, disciples, and juries! Thirteen? The devil's number. Like eleven, it breaks the perfection of twelve, as seven breaks the sequence of twelve's fractions. Thirteen at a table? Judas was a thirteenth and his Satanic act tied into Friday, the Friday on Skull Hill. Long before Judas, however, his number was baleful: therefore no thirteenth floor in a hotel, and Pew 12A in a church — and consternation if an unexpected quest arrives at a party of twelve. Yet thirteen colonies somehow succeeded.

Other superstitions show their vestigial survival, like the buttons on a man's coat sleeve from the time when he must fasten his cuff close on his wrist as protection from the elements. The horseshoe over the barn door, open end up so that the luck won't run out, puts in cold iron the outline of the blood-smeared hand of the threshold sacrificer above the door frame, protecting his home from the sword of the passing-over Angel of Wrath or announcing the bridal just consummated. Pennsylvania Dutch barns are painted with hex-medallions against the evil eye. If a black cat scuds across your path, turn back, because black cats belong to witches riding their broomsticks through the night sky to their tryst with Beelzebub — black cats stolen from Egypt's false gods. If you spill salt, quickly toss a pinch of it over your left shoulder, because every child born of woman is invisibly dogged from his birth by his bad angel behind his left shoulder, over against the good angel behind the right. Automatically, throw salt in the fiend's eyes to blind him. And why salt and all the ceremonial that has gone with it through the centuries? The cave men felt its mana, for it counteracts decay and preserves life: therefore it has deity in it.

Break a mirror? Seven years of bad luck — and why? Because, as the first puzzled possessors asked, if you see *yourself* in the mirror, aren't you somehow there and smitten by its smash? Cover the mirror in a death room so that there may be no entanglement of the departing person by its retaining glass. Tea-leaf readers, card fortunetellers, Gypsy palmists? They are shades of ancient augurs standing above crimsoned altars. Walk under a ladder? No, because the diagonal ladder, the ground, and the wall make a triangle, the sign of Trinity, which must not be brashly invaded.

Knock wood? Because it is in our blood from our earliest forebears who felt the mystery of nature's power and recognized the miracle in every bush " aflame with God." When they were betrayed into bumptiousness and, thumping their chest, boasted of their greatness, the cold chill of animist recollection suddenly prickled, so they reached over to the nearest embodiment of the Infinite and touched it to say, "Of course, by your leave." Wherefore we touch or knock wood to attest the humbling of our moment of vainglory to decent deference.

What minister would not wryly admit that the average

wedding is more compounded of superstition than it should be? The obligatory ritual is not only in the service's words but in "something borrowed, something blue and a sixpence (*not* a dime!) in her shoe" and all the other good luck magic of the whole procedure. Why? Because once on a time a prevalent certainty pictured the lovely maiden not only as desired by competing suitors but also as pursued by invisible spirits who were jealous that they had no embodiment in which they might join the contest. Therefore these jealous spirits, turned malevolent, must be thwarted of their evil conspiracy to wreck this wedding. The bride, swathed in a veil — opaque to camouflage her identity — must be surrounded by attractive girls, dressed identically, to bewilder the vicious spoilsports. The groom must be attended by identical groomsmen and, for safety, a "best man" must be named, to draw the ire of the ominous phantoms. And, lest there should be any warning of the wedding moment, the groom must *not* go near the bride on that day. Only when the hour had come would the groom's company dash out and seize the waiting damsel and carry her off. Something borrowed, to add *mana;* something blue, the Virgin's color, to get her sponsorship; a June wedding, if possible, because Juno (who had poor luck with her own marriage) presided over that month. The ring finger is the Amen finger, coming after Father, Son, and Holy Ghost; the left hand because it is connected most closely with the heart and the vein to the Amen finger. Old shoes, because in the olden time property was transferred after payment by the purchaser's putting his foot down on the property, even on his most valuable property, his bride's bowed head. Rice, either because it is the symbol of fertility or because the devilish spirits are so avaricious that they will stop to pick up the grains and lose the trail. The horseplay, sometimes very harsh, to prove to the ghouls that they needn't do anything, since all they could wish is already done.

There are superstitions galore, general or personally invented, but all either the parrying of bad luck or the insurance of good. The emotion that rules them is dread of the evil and hope of the good in spite of that evil. Numbed primitives lacked the confidence that, of its own strength, the divine could be counted on. Superstitions now have no such excuse, for our remote ancestors were fumbling for science but had not reached its assurance. Superstition is now both anti-realistic and anti-religious. It is the survival of fear. The more realistic faith, the less fear: the less faith, the more fear.

It is a long stretch from trust in the left hind foot of a rabbit that ran over the grave of a murderer at midnight in the dark of the moon — to Einstein, Jeans, Whitehead, Schweitzer, and Dewey, by way of Socrates, Spinoza, Buddha, Lao-tze, and Jesus. Yet our civilization covers it all.

CHAPTER EIGHT

Christianity and Non-Christian Faiths

In their original ideals the major non-Christian religions of the world are worthy of respect. They deserve to be estimated by the spirituality which their philosophic or mystic founders and true disciples exemplify. These ancient faiths are expressions of racial temperaments: therefore for their racial witness they merit open-minded study by Western society. In the democracy of all religious sincerities their ideologies have a just claim to be heard. No one but a bigot now scorns comparative religions.

Unfortunately for their genuine genius, the philosophic essentials of these faiths are cherished only by a small minority of their adherents. The preponderant majority of believers has been regrettably exploited by generations of manipulators and is now bound by superstition to practices which make us shudder. Yet, although these practices exceed even the grosser forms of orgiastic Christian perversion, it is not fair to forget that as the Christian churches would demand to be judged on the basis of their better forms, so these "heathen" religions should be appraised on their truer, purer concepts rather than on the pitiful credulity of the masses. Real Taoism has as much claim to be known through Lao-tze as Christianity has to be known by the actual religion of Jesus. Buddhism's standard is Gautama; Mohammedanism's is Mohammed; Hinduism's is in the Upanishads, the Rig-Veda, and in noblest Brahmanism. Before we sneer at the gong-banging, incense-burning, prayer-wheel-spinning, idol-worshiping, priest-and-caste-ridden customs which betray these essentially spacious, high faiths, we'd best examine our own house of faith.

To our chagrin, it is not conspicious that, pro rata, our religion has developed finer thinkers, more penetrative philosophers, or greater saints than these ancient faiths have produced. The consummate Taoist, Yogi, Brahmin, Confucian sage, or Mahayana Bodhisattva has a dignity of immemorial wisdom and a purity of dedicated life which puts to shame our energetic church leaders' standards of efficiency. In any notable proportion we are not growing the equivalent of gurus, Shangri-La lamas or Parsee illuminati. We should reverence the Zen Buddhist of Japan who, according to his thesis, concentrates above all else on the realization of the inmost self. The Tenri Shintoist preaches the Heavenly Reason as the sole supreme divinity and the quiet devotees of the Heavenly Reason prove its truths by what they are. What religion has more self-disciplinary rigor than the Mahayana disciple knows, who hopes to become in and of the universal Buddha that he may attain a crystalline, modest saviorhood in order to help others in their struggle?

The finer minority of each generic faith has kept itself clean of popular superstitions, and disdains pandering exploiters. Either by retiring into ascetic insulation where spiritual exercises are the regimen and deep mystical experience can be cultivated, or else by ashrams and other joint projects in which the study of other faiths may be joined with their own, the elite of these religions dissociate themselves from the tawdry vulgarity which defiles the name of their truth. These spiritual patricians of Eastern doctrine welcome the deeper thinkers of Western culture in the hope of that cross-fertilization of religions which should generate a "wholism" of new range and beauty.

Some day, please the God of all men, there should be a new Bible — a Bible of World Faith, in which the winnowed wisdom of all religions will find its legitimate place. There is a growing urgency for this, and many unofficial, conjectural compilations have been made experimentally. Except among obdurate hyperorthodox bibliolaters the acknowledgment that "God hath not left Himself without witness" is correcting the former superiority complex such as is typically symbolized by the timid mistranslation of bold Malachi's text into a diluted hope for the future. It should read: "From the rising of the sun even unto the going down of the same, My Name (i.e. Reality) *is* great among the Gentiles and in every place incense *is* offered unto Me and a pure offering; for My Name (Reality) *is* great among the 'heathen' saith the Lord of Hosts."

It is fascinating to hazard guesses as to the contents of a Bible of World Faith, such as would have the imprimatur of more than an individual scholar or publishing house. It is not a criticism of such pioneering compilations to dream of an ultimately standard Bible into which could go such portions of all scriptures as their own wisest, most discriminative proponents might select to present the gist of their highest thought. The most objective modernists of the varying cultures should be commissioned to winnow their scriptures and select their completely intrinsic and magnificent chapters. We of an alien race cannot evaluate them with such discrimination as their own meticulous selectors would exercise. We have our own big task for keen sensitivity — a task which must not merely force us to check on our Old and

New Testaments but must hold us to the even more discerning critique of additional religious classics which have become associate scripture. Our selective standards must be as fastidious as those which we require of our non-Christian confreres.

To undertake their book in the World Bible, aristocrats of Hinduism would have to sift the Rig-Veda hymns and the Atharva-Veda for their best psalm-equivalents. They should glean from the Upanishads the passages which give the purest speculations of the character of God and man's relation to him, and would pick out of the Lord's Song — the Bhagavad-gita — the words of life's meaning and death's. They must choose brief chapters of the knowledge of spirit as reality from Sankaracharya's Atma Bodha, from the Yoga Bodha, and from the Yogasutra the clues to meditation. One would hope also that some of Sri Ramakrishna's sage parables would be added as modern enrichment.

Fully equal to our Decalogue would be the Buddhist's Four Truths and the Noble Eightfold Path: 1. right belief; the recognition of truths about suffering; 2. right resolve; renouncing all evil purposes; 3. right speech; abstaining from lying, slandering, reviling, and idle talk; 4. right action; abstaining from taking or hurting life, from taking what is not given, and from carnal lust; 5. right livelihood; not following any occupation which takes unfair advantage; 6. right effort; to avoid and put away any evil state of mind and always to seek, cultivate, and cherish a good state of mind; 7. right mindfulness, self-possession which erases morbid longings and despondency; 8. right concentration; the stages of ecstacy in experience.

Certainly the Manual of Zen Buddhism would provide a magnificent section. The Analects of Confucius and the

Doctrine of the Steadfast Man would give many paragraphs, and the teachings of Mencius would be an accompaniment.

Above almost all other books in this hypothetical Testament would shine the Tao Tê Ching, the "Way" of Lao-tze.

The Zoroastrian Gathas and the Zend Avesta are a minor treasure trove; Mohammed's Alkoran and the Forty-Two Traditions of An-Nawawi might add a few verses.[1]

In the light of such a hypothetical anthology, on our own part and for our own good we might at once begin to assay our own scripture. Much of it is not worth saving. For all practical uses, most of the arid, outgrown, anti-spiritual portions of the Bible have already been eliminated. (Thomas Jefferson did this on his own, we remember.) There still would have to be a lot more weeding. By and by, however, the titanic authority of the prophets would be seen as pure genius and sheer moral heroism; the perfection of a top score of psalms would outshine the repetitious and cursing ones; the epic majesty of Job would be plain. Portions of the histories would be relevant. As to the New Testament, form-criticism must untangle historic data from myth in the Gospels; for the record of Jesus would get on much better without the miracles, the genealogies, the pretense of oracular divinity, and the fierce Apocalyptics of his day. He should be allowed to speak out and be cleanly understood, freed of the alien imputations foisted on him by special pleaders. *Christian* Christianity would be startlingly simple but startlingly challenging. Some of Paul's truths would emerge more appealingly once his casuistry and his mystery passion were screened out. We want I Corinthians 13, Ephesians 6, and Romans 8 (minus his predestination theory), and many other really constructive, well-loved passages. Hebrews and Revela-

---

[1] For all this, cf. Robert Ballou, *et al, The Bible of the World* (New York, 1939).

tion, however, proffer little which is not smothered in Temple analogies or Neronian Apocalyptics. At any cost, Jesus' unsullied ideals must be the principal contribution for us to render back to that Orient from which they arose.

But when one begins to speculate as to what should be in the further book of our Western genius, he is dazzled and dazed by the array of material which stretches from Marcus Aurelius to Einstein. Plato-Socrates, Euripides, Aeschylus, and Aristotle should have their say. A bit of Seneca and Augustine; certainly some strophes from Thomas a Kempis and some lyrics by Francis of Assisi; a sonorous cadence from Dante; a selection from wise old Maimonides; something pungent from John Bunyan; a page from John Woolman's *Journal*, from George Fox and Calvin and Wesley, perhaps from Jonathan Edward's philosophy (not his hell-fire sermons), certainly from Jefferson and Emerson and Parker, and so on. Any one person would be presumptuous to assume that he were competent to skim the cream of our spiritual heritage. But for inclusion in the World Bible we need something more compact than a Five-Foot Shelf or a Hundred Best Books for the mind and soul.

In a fair field with no favors there ought to be a survival of the fittest. Any evidence that other faiths need the fulfillment of their truths in the truth of humanity's birthright, of the kind of Christhood epitomized in the Carpenter of Nazareth, would place those other scriptures in a kind of "old testament," leading up to the clarified and expurgated "new" one. The estimate of greater truth would have to be won by fair demonstration of the quality of spiritual satisfaction and helpful life which it produced. We who have Christianity in our blood are instinctively champions for its pre-eminence, which sometimes tends to give us a superiority complex. But we are rocked back by the stern voice of realism which enunciates that we now must prove Christianity's right to a "new testament monopoly" solely by the caliber of character generated from its inspiration, a caliber so evident in our everyday existence among our fellows that they will want to share it.

No dictatorial or authoritarian "revelation" can now be tolerated. Bibliolators are vetoed by today's common sense. The only vindication for the Christian ethic is by giving most; not by demanding submission, but by losing itself to find itself in the larger synthesis. *Do even liberal Christians dare to say that they would be willing or happy that Christianity should lose its regal name and specific identity in a new, emergent world faith?*

As a postscript to the foregoing discussion of the world's religions, some consideration is called for of the missionary movement. What is the future of Christian missions?

Of course it has always been a caricature, except of the extremest fanatics, to picture the missionary as a black-coated foreigner on a soap box, orating to the heathen that their whole religion is of the devil, and that to be saved they must abandon their whole body of belief and submit to the "true faith," i.e., in the specific version of the sect which its emissary arbitarily presents.

Missions have been a strange mixture of heroism and essentially arrogant propaganda. Although individual missionaries — once in the field and in increasing touch with the finely bred top level leaders and also with the simpler, conditioned followers — have learned to respect and perhaps to love them, nevertheless, missions have represented a superiority complex. This has been a presupposed axiom, perhaps unspoken in bold crudity. No one can fail to feel the heroism and consecration which missionaries show by their sacrifice of home environment and their gift of themselves to far-flung endeavor. We give them credit for their real share in planting in these lands the concomitant benefits of education, medicine, agriculture methods, orphanages, social service, and the more civilized treatment of women. Whole communities, whole provinces, whole systems of indigenous society have been lifted by Christian schools and universities, medical centers, and hospitals, language projects, co-operatives, farming techniques, technologies, and other constructive agencies. These have been established and built up through eras of persecution, misunderstanding, famine, poverty, and war by missionaries who preached best by their zeal to be helpful. Sooner or later, those who came to know these ambassadors of the new faith felt their generosity in the name of a Master whose outstretched hand of blessing the missionaries felt themselves to be, where need was at its crucial maximum. But to thoughtful natives the salvation which was proffered via the churches remained a magic they could not comprehend. To the childlike it remained a magic to replace the ancestral one, possibly better, certainly backed by Western civilization's prestige, and therefore worth weighing.

Up to and until the revolution in the Near and Far East, missions were somewhat emerging from their policy of spiritual sovereignties and colonialism. The perpetuation of fundamentalist programs seemed weakened. The competition between rival infallibilities, except that between Catholic and Protestant, was starting to give way to comity of practice. It was to be expected that the Roman Church must inflexibly continue its assumption of exclusive authority from on High and, despite the compromise of a few native bishops, that all converts must look to His Holiness in the far-off Vatican as their extraterritorial commander. Parallel to this extraterritorial sovereignty, fervent sectarians expected their disciples to feel allegiance to the home church and its board of missions. The official doctrine was an imported one. There was more than a joking illustration in the report of a New Englandish meeting house on a side street in Hankow, emblazoned with a big sign, "The Two Seed in the Spirit American Reformed Church of China." How could any Oriental, coolie or not, thread his way to the Son of Man through the maze of a subdivisional American adaptation of a fragment of Protestantism divided from other Protestantism by the subtle metaphysic of election which was a part of the rebellion against the medieval Roman Church of European history from apostolic primitivism? Yet this indicates the literal missionary polity.

Although this polity was fading, the criterion of success was "How many converts?" Other objectives were secondary. "Rice Christians" have been too numerous and too welcome, because statistics of conversions were needed to keep support coming. The home office held the reins tight, keeping title to the mission properties, allocating expenditures from headquarters according to overseas direction. In many cases the church disregarded the wishes of appeasement which the emissaries on location knew were justified. Reactionaries who held the purse strings were suspicious that, given freedom, missionaries might relax dogmatic rigidity and become chameleonlike on heathendom. No, fundamentalism had to be undeviating and Western!

The opposite policy was gaining, however, among the more liberal minority abroad. There was a groundswell against sectarian rivalry and against occidental jots and tittles.

The broader-minded missionaries (and some home boards under their pressure) had seen the unwisdom of competition and gradually had wrought out co-operative plans, generously accrediting each other's worth. The home directors developed more and more trust in their agents abroad. Most sanely, among the newer attitudes, the frank acknowledgment of the virtues of the indigenous faiths was flowering in a will to aid native genius to develop its own type of Christianity out of what was seen to be an "old testament" of its own.

The leadership in this sounder program was first of all in the younger churches, foreseeing eventual self-direction by natives. Federated unity, more elastic and gracious than the home churches yet dared for themselves, was in wider scope. The United Church of South India is the best example. It is the finest venture of unity in the whole non-Christian world. Created by the initiative of the late Bishop Azariah of Dornakal, an Indian, uniting the Methodists, Presbyterians, and Anglicans there, this inclusive Indian Church has not been validated by the parent communions in England. The Lambeth Council of Anglican Bishops, for instance, has deferred to "the substantial minority which could not recognize its orders" but embarrassedly "blesses it and prays for its restoration of communion with the Church," now forfeited! The magic idea still binds.

And this despite the trust felt for the truly great men and women of those younger churches. Men, like Jimmy Yen, Toyohiko Kagawa, T. Z. Koo, and Azariah are arguments for trust. Yet Albert Schweitzer, of all men, was forbidden to preach or teach, when he went to Africa, because he is a heretic! He had to get his own funds for Lambarene. And

Gandhi was looked at askance by the illiberals, because, although he studied and practiced the Gospel ideas, he was no "Christian"!

World War II was a catastrophe to the missionary movement. The transition to autonomous native churches was in progress except among die-hards. Japan and India and China were soon to see foreign missionaries withdrawn, said missionary optimists, except for specialists requested in advisory capacity for technical skills. Native administrators were already taking over from their former teachers, who gladly demoted themselves.

But do not forget, even this trend was *inside* the orthodox churches. The creed of a magic Christianity, though less openly stressed by semi-liberals, remained the norm of doctrine.

Then came the sweep of world revolution. Is anyone so obstinately unawakened as not to sense its tidal wave? Noah's flood was nothing to this. The revolution that has begun is greater than the ending of the Roman Empire. It is wider, deeper, and more searching. The peoples of the world are on the march. Across the globe everywhere, human society is seething with change. If India should go Communist, two-thirds of the human race would be under the dictatorship of the Kremlin. And where is religion in the maelstrom? Religion cannot follow Voltaire's advice to those who live in an agonizing era, to dig in their own walled garden. Established religion is finding the walls of its garden battered down. Even while terrified religionists cling closer to other-worldly authority, their authority itself is under threat.

This is not the place to discuss the over-all aspects of the insurrection of today's sans-culottes. For this chapter is dealing only with the limited subject which might well be called *ex*-missions. Yet in the total mutiny by the many, the fate of missions is included. Missions are pictured by the malcontents as an element in the colonialism they hate. No matter how self-sacrificial the evangelists may have been, the devastating fact for them is that the tide of the times is pulling the sand from under the feet of any unrealistic theological theory and practice. Missions may survive in comparably insulated spots and the revolutionaries may gladly take over their medical and educational adjuncts, but straight-out preaching of Revelation according to Conformity is scorned. Although missions' advocates may tighten their belts and cry out that the other name for crisis is challenge, in secret there must be consternation. The Church Militant's creedal sorties into "heathen" faiths have met militant opposition.

Three hundred million Moslems from Egypt, Morocco, Iran, Iraq, Turkey, Arabia and the rest of the Middle East, to Afganistan, Pakistan, Indonesia, Java, Malaya and the Philippines, demand the right of self-determination. And this demand is as much religious as nationalistic. The political issues are so intense because Mohammedanism is a passionate faith. Christian missions, never really successful against Islam, are now apparently being swept out, along with the economic oligarchs of colonialism.

India may present a complex problem to the Western world but underneath all the cultural variations, ranging from orgiastic idolatries to the noble philosophy of the Brahmin sages, there is one underlying psychological attitude toward life which is categorically Hindu. The Hindu temperament is quite different from the Anglo-American, and now that India has self-government, "Swaraj" inevitably includes repudiation of the religion of the former overlord.

Gandhi proved and Nehru knows that Europe is not in the world's saddle any longer, and American ideology is alien. Satyagraha pits soul-force against the white man's ascendancy. Even though Christian missions mushroomed by their welcome to untouchables, that prestige was dissipated by Gandhi's championship of his Harijans; and the relaxation of the caste system has further lessened the missionary advantage. Hinduism has been brought to a new level of legitimate pride by its pre-eminent interpreters in literature and international policy. Vedanta is on a new level. A Christianity touched with British influence has but a remote chance of being considered divinely revealed and final. Its *mana* is fading.

In Red China Christian missions are gone. So also, one fears, Confucianism, Buddhism, and Taoism have lost potency. The Communist scorn for religion strikes a death blow to the Christian evangel's proclamation.

The situation in Japan is more problematic. It is self-evident that Christianity, as the nominal religion of Nippon's conquerors, may indeed have had the momentary advantage of the occupation, but what will be the fate of that faith when Japan is actually its own master again? The *Bushido* of the samurai and the once prevailing slogan, "Japan for the Japanese" are still in the blood of the present generation. The religion of an America which used atom bombs to gain a victory cannot enjoy unalloyed deference. A new version of political Shinto may well be the orthodoxy of the Sunrise Kingdom, particularly if it proves imperative in combating the wiles of Communism.

Traditional Christianity is plunged into the crucible of the world revolution. There is no divine right of sovereignty for missionary polity which will be accepted on any major scale in the Near or Far East, or among the insurgent peoples anywhere. The churches' magic is denied as political extra-territorialisms pass.

Is it fantastic to dream that someday all the faiths can inspire each other? This may come about when the leaders of the world's great religions emphasize their simple common principles and discard the magic ritual of supernatural sanction.

An Interpolated Note

With Chapter Nine this book takes a new direction. Its case thus far has been the analysis of religion *with magic,* to prove how far the ideology of magic has permeated organized religion. Now it is time to turn to constructive considerations, to see what religion can be *without magic.*

The preceding sketches of magicized religion have been as drastic as the author feels they should be without too monotonous a shredding and itemized documentation for every minute point. His hope has been that if some hesitant liberals still within the toils of reactionary institutionalism will read these challenges with wrenched-open minds, they will be brought to objectivity and realization of their timidness. If a few conservatives, bred in the belief that there can be nothing worthy of the name of religion which is not guaranteed by the miraculous, could be brought to the point where they would take seriously this sincere and critical diagnosis, then let them squarely answer its arguments. Can they justify their concept of Christ, salvation, grace, sacraments, miracle, the Cross, and the Judgment by any proof which will stand up under test? Let sentimentalists analyze the piety which has held them fast. And if any of these paragraphs seem unduly fiery, let them turn, for instance, to Amos, Micah, Jeremiah, Isaiah, and Matthew 23—and, no longer at a safe distance from the institutionalism they pilloried, read the devastating Biblical indignation it merited and still merits. Listen:

"Now, O ye priests, this command is for you. If ye will not hear and if ye will not lay it to heart . . . I will even send a curse on you and will spread dung upon your faces, even the dung of your solemn feasts, and one shall take you away with it. . . . Ye have departed out of the way, ye have caused many to stumble at the law; ye have corrupted the Covenant. Thus saith the Lord."[1]

Or, once more: "I hate, I despise your solemn feasts and your solemn assemblies. . . . And I will turn your feasts into mourning and all your songs into lamentation. . . . Behold, the days come, saith the Lord God, that I will send a famine into the land, not a famine of bread nor a thirst for water, but of hearing the words of the Lord."[2]

Or in the words of Jesus to the nation's legalists: "Woe unto you, scribes and Pharisees, hypocrites! For ye shut up the kingdom of heaven against men and ye neither go in yourselves, neither suffer ye them that would enter to go in. . . . Woe unto you, scribes and Pharisees, hypocrites! For ye pay tithe of mint and anise and cummin and have omitted the weightier matters of the law; judgment, mercy and faith. . . . Whited sepulchres . . . blind guides . . . Ye compass sea and land to make one proselyte, and when he is made ye make him twofold more the child of hell than yourselves. . . . Children of them that killed the prophets . . . Ye serpents, ye generation of vipers, how can you escape the damnation of hell?"[3]

These are not very gentle words, are they? There are many more just as searing. There is precedent, you see, for identical indignation when identical evils are rediscovered.

---

[1]Malachi 2:1-3, 8.
[2]Amos 5:21; 8:10a, 11.
[3]Matthew 23 passim.

Humanity is so sacred that any treachery to it is intolerable.

Therefore the latter portion of this book must be devoted to an investigation of what religion can be when it is without magic. The parable of the exorcised devil and the swept and garnished empty house is inescapable. Exorcise magic but leave religion empty of spirituality and the seven devils of materialism, license, and bumptious power will slyly take over. When it emerges from captivity, pure religion shines with uncontaminated simplicity.

As a structural framework of one individual's unofficial but sincere religion without magic—as far as he can divest it of the faintest remnants of that obsession—here is the hazarded epitomization of *a* faith, for whatever it may have of suggestion to others for theirs.

Lest we succumb to mere negatives, we must discipline ourselves to the much harder task of positives. A rebellion may win freedom, but what do freed people do with their freedom? The responsibility for the noble use of liberty is then upon them. Gospel stories of healings by Jesus too frequently close with some remark such as "He took him and healed him and let him go." We never hear of the healed man or woman again, tied into discipleship. We who want religion healed of its sickness must demonstrate to ourselves and others what a life there is ahead for healed faith.

Any "faith" which remains what one does not believe is hardly a faith. Perhaps we may only win a new beginning for our cleared-up faith, but at the very least we should be able to say, "This one thing I know, that whereas I was blind, now I see!"

BOOK TWO

RELIGION WITHOUT MAGIC

CHAPTER NINE

Half-Liberals and Honest Doubt

Perhaps enough has been said in the preceding pages to indicate that among all the men and women who are aligned with the Christian Church for good or ill, half-liberals are in the most uncomfortable and untenable position of all.

Fundamentalists are militantly sure of themselves: they are dead certain that their respective literalist beliefs—or credulities—have incontrovertible scriptural infallibility.

On the other hand, agnostics are free from uneasy compromise with creeds. They may have come to their agnosticism through disillusionment and strain, but when their doubts have hewn away untenable ideology, they are stable in their few modest certainties. They pretend no esoteric revelation about that which is beyond the immediate horizon of the human mind and heart; they leave the Infinite in its mystery.

Materialists are also consistent in their beliefs; they are smug and sure in their easy thing-mindedness. They shrug off the problem of the spiritual as not worth bothering over. They are too well-heeled or too busy in hand-to-mouth subsistence to waste time on what they consider the vaporous myths of religion. They may have a repertoire of arguments against the "Mistakes of Moses" and miracles, which they repeat like a worn phonograph record if religion is mentioned; they dismiss the whole hypothesis by some bromide which, if true at all, applies only to some surface detail of a pre-Victorian stereotype religion. They are comfortably sure of themselves.

But half-liberals are *not* comfortable or sure of themselves or free from compromise. Their consciences are uneasy in proportion as their minds are in ferment. They are nervous. They are secretly suspicious that their rationalizing does not hold truth. Nevertheless they still join in saying the creeds (or at least stand up when the creeds are said) and *appear* to be orthodox; and, although with lagging steps, they still march in the institutional ranks. Because of their souls' disquiet, they deserve pity.

What is this rationalizing process? Casuistry is the defensive art of making erroneous or specious positions appear to be sound. It weaves a spider web of plausibility around sheer dishonesty. Sophists are not all dead; they have outlived classic Greece. Half-liberals might well reread Aristophanes' *Clouds,* for the Church has become their "thinkery" and they, not Socrates, are suspended in their basket of "Interpretation."

Let's see how their standard dialectic works. First, what do the rationalizers say of the ancient creeds in a modern age? Their special pleading goes something like this:

"The historic creeds are not categorical statements of literal doctrine in the merely dictionary sense of their words. *They are not a map of the faith: they are its flag.* A map is only flat geography, but a flag is the proud symbol of a nation's life! We do not hold the faith: the faith holds *us* by the living truth which no words can more than suggest. It is the faith which the words carry as the eagle's wings carry the eagle. After all, remember that words are only semantic sounds to which we give an agreed meaning. The connoted meaning is the important thing. All right then, the words of the creeds are not like ordinary prose words; they are mystically sacramental with the life-in-faith which comes streaming down through the centuries from its fountainhead, the outward and audible signs of an inward and spiritual grace given to us. The Church is a single life, embodied in the successive generations exactly as a nation is a single life, not its momentary aggregate of citizens. The creeds begin, 'I believe,' yet the 'I' is not the individual who speaks it at the moment; it is the Church now using his lips, tongue, and heart to affirm its changeless testimony to the majesty and inspiration of the divine. To reduce the creeds to the level of their mere words would be to lose the inexpressible, mystical life they hold."

Said with sufficient intensity and in habitual chorus with sufficient numbers of others who like the feeling of an act of togetherness, such rationalization can smother that inconvenient still small voice which insists that words mean what they say, first, last, and always, and in their scrupulous basic exactitude. Any such tongue-fencing as the foregoing is of course not consciously used by the whole Church membership. Generally, people take the creeds in their stride as a rote incidental which arouses no mental disquiet and causes no logical dilemma. It is only the objective half-realists who are stung by the gadfly of a more drastic honesty.

Here is another example of the rationalist's hedging as he tries to meet the common objection to the Virgin Birth doctrine, that it is opposed to reason and science. The more erudite of these skeptics are armed with historic data that Jesus' fatherless begetting was a borrowed bit of mythology current among most Mediterranean and Indian peoples to buttress the role of their own divine saviors. The uncomfortable clericalist hastily alleges:

"The method of Christ's birth is not essential. The essential is the fact of the incarnation. The ancient Christians were trying to express the fact of the Incarnation, which is that the God-man, who is the fullness of the Godhead bodily, is not explainable by any process of biologic generation, but is given us from above by God's own initiative. He who believes in the incarnation can therefore say its conveying words of the virgin birth with such mental reservations as he personally may feel about their reportorial accuracy, because the pivotal faith of the incarnation is affirmed by them. That is the agreed inner meaning, you see."

So much for creedal "interpretations." Yet there is a deeper incongruity—that of the hypothesis of the Incarnate One in magic action in a world of natural law and human life.

What has been done by the dogmatists to the Carpenter of Nazareth and his truly religious religion? His own contempories, alas, were not the only "wicked and adulterous generation seeking a Sign," i.e., an authentication by magic. The divine nature ascribed to him by the subsequent Church gave to him a masquerading omnipotence impossible to integrate with human nature. The trick device of the "two natures" is an explanation which does not explain him in any psychological way. His consequent sinlessness, miracles, transfiguration, atoning cross, physical resurrection, and bodily ascension are of a piece with virgin-birth origin— equally unreal. By what ear to heaven or factual proof do the dogmatists foist on the Church the pre-existence of a Christ who is timeless, eternal, omnipotent, omniscient, absolute, universal, completely all that God was, is, and shall be, the second Person of the Trinity, who by his own volition "emptied himself" of his supernatural, transcendent powers and descended out of the glory in the heaven of heavens, taking on the envelope of that helpless babe of Bethlehem, virgin-born, in a stable in a meager little province of a long-dead empire?

The metaphysic which rests on the incarnation, so defined, works out into that of the atonement, by which the embodied "God out of God," despised and rejected and crucified by blind pawns of Satan, accomplishes the world-changing act by which the Almighty somehow exploits His Son (who is himself), as the Lamb slain from the foundation of the world, enabling him to give his grace to the elect of all time and to "justify" them unto salvation. What a phantasmagoria both of logic and of morals!

Calvary thus becomes the neck of the hourglass of all human and divine destiny, the focus of all evolution in the universe since the day of Creation up through all human history. From the Cross flows out all the redemption which men can gain by acceptance of its vicarious bloodshed. The Saving Victim opens wide the gate of heaven to fallen sons and daughters of Adam and Eve, provided they are "elect." How? No logical explanation of *how* is available; we must accept the inscrutable fact and be plunged in the fountain filled with blood drawn from Emmanuel's veins.

Then, unbelievably, this Aladdin's lamp theory of the Cross proceeds into the postscriptive proof that Christ had been God's other self, by the resuscitation of his corpse and its bodily sublimation by the ascension into heaven, back into timeless glory, to watch from his throne at the right hand of the Father, between the cherubim. There he watches the working out of the grace now committed to the Church as its endowment of regenerative wonder-working, until that ordained but secret moment in celestial time which is his cue for cataclysmic return to earth. The thunder clouds will then dart their bolts of lightning, there will be a blasting earthquake, the graves will open and give up their dead, and the Last Assize will mete out hell or heaven to the quick and dead.

Isn't this incredible? Yet it is the never-repudiated doctrine into which the tale of the itinerant Prophet of Nazareth has been twisted. The foregoing paragraphs are an unexaggerated summary of it. *This is the orthodox creed.* When put into its unvarnished idiom, it is nothing less than shocking. It is shocking for its contradiction of helpful spirituality and for its unfounded sophistry. Seen nakedly, it shocks the timid half-modernists and secretly liberal religionists who have glossed over its moral ugliness and glamorized its grotesqueness until they have nearly forgotten how fantastic the skeletal scheme is. They hastily disavow their implicit acceptance of such phrasing and wall themselves inside their own equivocations. If they are ever taxed with the inconsistency of their position they have to admit that they swallow the articles of belief with many grains of salt. If they are frank with themselves they know that although they are counted in the registered battalion of the faith, they are now thrust out into a kind of no man's land between fallacy and fact, exposed to crossfire from both sides.

Few such men and women really let go of the magic which inheres in their tradition. Although they dwell on Jesus' complete humanity they cannot cease to think of him as a marionette Savior whose voice is God's own.

As long as the writhing body hangs on Catholic and neo-Catholic altars, as long as that tortured, haloed figure shines from the nimbus of standardized windows, as long as the sign of the cross is made with some notion that it cabalistic-

ally blesses, as long as the sacred scapular, medal, amulet, or
cross is worn as the holy equivalent of a rabbit's foot, as long
as prayers are not thought influential unless they bring in
Jesus' name for their imprimatur, just so long are believers
under the spell from which courage should salvage them.
The soldiers stripped Jesus of the scarlet robe and crown of
thorns which they had put on him to caricature him as a
mock king, and "they put his own raiment on him" to lead
him away. With opposite feeling for him, brave champions
of him as he truly was and is strip him of the panoply of
false theorizing and lead him *in his own clothes* not to Golgotha but away into vital, human comradeship with the disciples of rigorous truth.

Religious liberalism is also arrestingly challenged by the
subtle and eloquently advocated doctrine of Neo-Orthodoxy.
Neo-Orthodoxy addresses itself precisely to those semi-liberals
who, although they are restless over the archaic ideology of
the churches, are nevertheless still church members. Its credo
begins with even more sweeping strictures on contemporary
ecclesiasticism than the semi-liberals themselves have dared to
voice; but then it proceeds to a deeper fundamentalism than
is usually affirmed even by reactionaries. The attack on
churchly and secular assumptions is relentless. By its bril-
liant acumen and one-sided selectivity it amasses an impressive array of evidence against the modern world and its institutions; then it reverts to a supernatural solution. Yet the
momentum gained by the initial critique of our era is so im-
pelling that many an endorser of it is carried on into bewildered acquiescence.

Dr. Reinhold Niebuhr and Dr. Paul Tillich of the Union
Theological School are the shapers of this American thesis.

Somewhere in the background are cloudy Kierkegaard and Karl Barth of the "Wholly Other" God doctrine, and so too are Schopenhauer, Freud, Spengler, and Toynbee. By his supple mind and his personal magnetism, Dr. Niebuhr has indoctrinated a generation of young theologs (it being said that no student can graduate from Union until he has learned to love his Niebuhr as himself), a wide university circle, and the far-flung audience which has heard his notable preaching. In his own right, Dr. Tillich is an able co-advocate. Neo-Orthodoxy is aimed at high-level moderns who despair of the present era. And there are many such.

Reduced to its skeletal outlines, what is Neo-Orthodoxy?

As indicated above, it is an indictment of so-called civilization: all men are sinners. On the sordid, evil side it is easy to build a damning case against our society by adding up its war horrors and psychoses, its exploitings, racisms, communisms, absolutisms, criminalities, perversions, delinquencies, and other iniquities. They are all too true. But Neo-Orthodoxy is not content with such facile summaries; it has something more unexpected and more soul-searching to say to "good" people. They too are sinners if they have any tinge of hope or confidence that their struggle for self-realization is valid. For in proportion as they are reliant on their innate powers they are victims of sinful pride. Faith in human potentialities results, says Dr. Niebuhr, in "a sweat of self-righteousness" which is the most devastating of all the sins. All frank liberalism, science, and humanistic faith breed "vainglory." Self-trust and attempts at self-fulfillment by merely human endeavor are anti-religious — "man makes himself God."

By examples—other than of personal travail—the case against pride is built up to show the egotism of national and international power politics and the egotism of the Church. "The world no longer accepts the essentials of the Christian faith." Secularism, it seems, is a reaction against a profane Christianity; it has been "forced to resist a profanization of the holiness of God both in the realm of truth and in the realm of the good, in both culture and ethics. . . . A profanization of the holiness of God leads inevitably to an effort to eliminate the sacred from human life."

All peoples and their institutions are therefore under God's judgment. "The divine word of judgment is spoken against the whole human enterprise." In its abandonment of true faith our age is on the road to doom. The judgment of God is shown in the downfall of civilizations and empires—our own civilization perhaps to be included. "Every humanistic creed is a cosmos of meaning sustained by a thin ice on the abysmal deeps of meaninglessness and chaos!"

The parable of the prodigal son is aptly applicable. "The more rationalistic humanism is the son in the first stages of his emancipation from his father. . . . Our civilization did not want to recognize its dependence upon a divine father, who is the source of all life and the judge of all human actions. It wanted an autonomous culture. . . . The more romantic type of modern humanism, as revealed in the religio-political movements of the Continent, represents a more advanced state of disintegration. Here the son is 'wasting his substance in riotous living,' a civilization . . . insisting that any vital or unique energy is morally self-justifying. The 'mighty famine' when the son begins to be in want is still in the future, but our civilization is destined for such a catastrophe as so certain a consequence of the anarchy of its conflicting national passions and ambitions." Therefore the prodigal must return in utter penitence to the father whose wisdom is "beyond human knowledge but not contrary to human experience." The *Dies Irae* echoes again.

So far, this is a searching, though extremist, argument. But what is the Neo-Orthodox solution? The solution is, in effect, sheer supernaturalism. Since man is hoist by his own petard and can do nothing by his own powers to save himself, he must come to God with complete repentance and cry for the grace from on high which alone can be his salvation. "The fulfillment of life, according to our Christian faith, is only possible through the mercy of God." Only God has self-reliance; man has none. God's gift of himself is realized only by those who repent of their self-trust. "Our gospel is one that assures salvation in the Cross of Christ to those who heartily repent of their sins. It is a gospel of the Cross; and the Cross is a revelation of the love of God only to those who have first stood under it as a judgment. . . . It is in the Cross that we become conscious how, not only what is worst but what is best in human culture and civilization is involved in Man's rebellion against God. . . . The world is redeemed by Him. Without His grace mediated through Christ, human existence remains a problem to itself, being unable to escape by any effort of its own from the contradictions of a sinful existence."[1]

Neo-Orthodoxy *fundamentally* is a version of magic Messianism. But those who believe there is no magic to be wrought by repentance and grace must as believers in human life take up man's burden of responsibility, believing that righteousness *has* a chance to triumph in this world. The Supreme Life exists on earth in the measure that life and struggle become meaningful.

---

[1]Quotations from Dr. Niebuhr given here are all from the final essay "The Christian Church in a Secular Age" in his *Christianity and Power Politics* (New York, 1940).

Neo-Orthodoxy ends in unrealism, discouraging earnest struggle for human ends. It is only the old, old orthodoxy, neo-ly redone.

Laymen who are half liberal may feel little pressure against equivocation. But if the half-liberal happens to be a cleric, he feels obliged to increase his self-extenuations to justify the expediency of his compromises. For the clergy are called to more accurate thinking than are layfolk and they are supposed to have the courage of deeper conviction. Yet the average non-fundamentalist minister is in a predicament; by his ordination vows, he is pledged to the official faith in its official form. He is the servant of the institution, he has a family to support by his profession, he has natural ambitions for betterment, and he must show results by his ability to build up his parish and its support of the official cause. He had best not wound the peace of mind of backbone parishioners who probably want what they call the simple gospel, which means "No theology and no personal applications that are too specific." He remembers the classic story of the tycoon who stamped out of church muttering, "Things have come to a pretty pass when religion interferes with a man's private life!" It is a line of least resistance for the rationalizer to extenuate any cowardice by telling himself that he can do more good through the constituted machinery than by throwing away his chance to bore from within. He repeats to himself that there are plenty of safe sermons that he can honestly preach, avoiding controversial ground. The services he conducts can be trusted to be so dignifiedly impressive that his congregation will be carried safely past the archaisms in the liturgy and he can manipulate selections and intercessions to sidestep most debatable points. And he can live out his true religion in his pastoral contacts. He will be judged by the practical and compassionate good he does for his flock. So he can reason. Half-liberal laymen and laywomen haven't a fraction of his excuse, nor does it take a fraction of his courage to burn their bridges, for most modern layfolk are alike in their prerogative to take or leave this or that incidental of the faith as they choose, though there are many who choose to be done with compromise.

For some timid liberals the strain grows importunate. The urge to honesty gnaws at their stamina. Insistent scruples are like corks in the water which can be kept under the surface only by tiring pressure. The instant there is weariness, doubts bob to the surface and float there defiantly. Some day, let us hope, something will snap inside the timid liberal's will and he will stand up, square his shoulders—and Mr. Facing-Both-Ways will be no more.

Nothing truly vital stays as it was. If life is not continually more abundant, it has already begun to die. So it is with convictions. Religious doubt, when it is sincere and inescapable, is only the negative side of a faith too deep for comfort inside the narrow definitions of a creed. It breaks the eggshell of old-time formal beliefs by incubated integrity.

If, as Gerald Heard defines it, "faith is the resolve to give the highest possible meaning to all we know," it is inevitable that with new facts continually being added to our knowledge, faith must face them and transcend with a richer truth the narrower beliefs once held. As was said before, if the dogmas of a previous day, when there was less knowledge and less of a scientific spirit, must be taken as set with changeless fixity for all time, then creedal religion is sure to be left behind as knowledge expands and is transformed by unforeseen new discoveries.

Honest doubt deserves none of the scorn with which outraged conformists anathematize it, forgetting the "Friend of sinners" who was *the* non-conformist of his day. The doubter has faith in the larger reality.

Questioning comes from an intuition of something greater than former codifications. At first the negative certainty may be more emphatic than the positive one to come; for shackles must be broken before a stride forward can be taken. There may be an empty moment when the comfortable old form is gone and the doubter may gasp, "They have taken away my assurance and I know not where they have laid it!" But out of the haze there presently comes the shape of a personal faith more satisfying to the growing mind.

Many years ago Dr. John Kelman the Scotsman was talking to college men about doubt. His address ran something as follows: "As I cross your American campuses I am amused to see so many of you carrying a gold-headed cane. I know why you do it. You do it to persuade yourselves you're grown up. You have your doubts if you are and need the reassurance of appearances to impress yourself and others. As I talk with some of you, I find you are carrying a mental gold-headed cane, and for the same reason. You think you are not grown up if you don't pretend you have doubts. With such men I have small patience. But if you are the kind that are dragged into doubting by your own questioning honesty, I've something very definite to say which you may not expect. It's this; if you cannot *help* doubting, *don't stop!* Doubt everything you can. Keep on. Be faithful at it. Bye and bye you'll come to something you cannot doubt. It may be only that the sun's going to rise tomorrow morning. But when you come to something you cannot doubt, stand up on your own two feet and say, 'I believe.' You're out of the negative into the positive. You've the nub of a belief. But *then* don't stop. Say to yourself, 'What does that imply? The sun's going to rise? Regularity! Regularity is dependability. Dependability is Law. Law has a cause.' . . . On you go. Bye and bye you'll have a faith back. It won't wear the old clothes. It won't prate the old words. But by the living Lord, you'll have the right to use the first person singular pronoun when you say 'I believe!' "

No sincere agnostic is arrogant; neither is he cowardly. He does not start with categorical assumptions of infinite ultimates and work backward to the familiar and specific. He begins with what he can actually know, and goes outward to the utmost of that data. All agnostics have *some* clear faith at the center of the circle of facts of which they are sure, but beyond that spotlighted center what is as yet unknown is still shrouded in the fog. The agnostic never says he disbelieves in what the fog may shroud. He modestly says, "I don't know what is there, and I make no presumptuous assertions about what I don't know."

For some agnostics the lighted area is larger than it is for others. Yet in every case its central area is experienced fact and the logical deductions only from fact.

The central area of certitude is at least Humanist. For we know our own and our neighbor's inherent nature and its motivations by inside information. Everyone takes our human nature as his first axiom, whether or not he has thought through its immediate meaning. Despite all the apparently contrary exceptions, we believe in Man. Even if credence is no more that this confident faith in humanness, it is religious. It may not presume anything at all about God, yet it is still an honest faith.

Dr. John Dietrich, the Humanist, says, "Only so far as religion concentrates its worship on Reality — things as they are — has it any saving power. For if we are really earnest for human life, if we see it for the frail thing that it is, dependent for its security, its happiness, even its existence, upon obedience to the laws of life, how can we be supremely concerned about anything but this obedience? A religion that will teach us how to live, that will hold up high and clear the laws of life and win our obedience to them, a religion that will develop the proper emotional response to the universe as we now know it to exist — that is the religion the world needs, and it is the only worthwhile religion. *One does not have to believe in God to be religious."* [2]

Some of us who agree with the honesty voiced in such agnosticism may wish that its deductions could proceed on and up. But we bow to its integrity. Its estimate of human values and qualities is impressive. There is reverence in Humanism along with its warmhearted emphasis on common traits.

Other agnostics push their deductions *beyond* the Humanist minima. They are in similar case with the scientists who know electricity by what it does, but cannot know what electricity is in itself. Humanists study humans and know that some mysterious force, not merely mechanical, makes them tick as they do. They wish they could waive the traditional, glib name for it — God. The name *God* carries such overtones of a supernaturalism so scientifically alien and so philosophically narrow that its implications are too petty. Since names are only containers usually filled with what-

[2]From a sermon delivered at Minneapolis and published by the First Unitarian Society there, 1937.

ever ideas have been associated with them, the name of God is impossible for these Humanists and they fumble for some new name which can be filled with that greater significance which they discern. They know that human motivations come from and point to an explanatory over-life. They know the metes and bounds of their own convictions, and within those widening limits they *believe*. They are Humanists-plus.

Such agnostics tend toward Theism — sound Theism. And they are truly eager to welcome the Carpenter of Nazareth for the light he can shed on the *plus factor*. For his philosophy was based on man's unspoiled nature. His axioms were good will, compassion, hope, courage, charity, love, and self-giving, for which he demanded unlimited application in all mutual relations. For him, one recognizes, religion was Humanism-plus. It leavened his life into beauty and strength. He was no codal robot for the ecclesiasts' absentee Landlord and inscrutable Lawgiver — wrathful if disobeyed, won to favoritism by meek serfdom. *Do you recall how seldom Jesus used the name "God"?* He preferred Humanist synonyms like "our Father." When he was queried about his ideas of God he almost invariably replied by evidential analogies of human traits, saying, *"What man of you,* having a hundred sheep and one goes astray . . ." or "What man shall there be among you, if his son ask bread. . . ." Or he told the parable of the Prodigal Son's father and of the Good Samaritan to show that the natural motives of unspoiled men and women are the divine in them.

Doubt is needed. Agnostic honesty opens up scientific religious investigation. It clears out the weeds, and gives room for good grain to spring up. How much more to be honored are brave explorers of reality than are inhibited semi-liberals, choked by expediency.

CHAPTER TEN

Is the Bible Outmoded?

In your grandparents' home there probably were two Bibles. One was Grandfather's. The other was Grandmother's. At least, this is typical.

Grandfather's Bible was on the marble topped center table in the front parlor. It must have weighed nine pounds. It had carved leather covers and heavy paper pages, including the stiffer ones of the illuminated Family Record, in which Grandfather inscribed marriages, births, and deaths. There were Doré engravings at crucial chapters. Its frontispiece was of the Tables of the Commandments, haloed by lightnings, with the Hebrew letters of Jehovah's name written on the thunderclouds.

Between Sundays this Bible rested in the fast-shut front room, where the atmosphere always seemed of bated breath. The window curtains were drawn within six inches of the sills. The closed square piano suggested an ebony coffin, adorned with its velvet shroud and its vase of pampas grass plumes. Haircloth chairs stood in funereal precision against the baseboards. The family's museum exhibits on the fluted shelves of the corner whatnot defied familiar handling.

Each Sunday—which grandfather persisted in calling the Sabbath—when he had taken his forty winks alone in this sanctum of awe, you were summoned into the musty room and climbed silently onto a slippery chair to give ear to word from Horeb. His white beard keeping time with his enunciation, Grandfather read his selected chapter from the ominous Book. Perhaps mistakenly, memory says that the chapter was usually some formidable one from Lamentations or Revelation; yet in that setting even the Sermon on the Mount would have seemed threatening. At other times Grandfather was a quiet, gentle man. It was only when he became major-prophetic that his blue eyes flashed and his voice took on Apocalyptic rumblings.

Grandmother's Bible was different. It lay on the big kitchen table, on the red checked tablecloth, either under or on her cookbook, along with her overflowing basket of mending. Its limp covers were more limp by much handling. Its pages fell open at the favorite chapters of her Bible within the Bible, marked with loose clippings which had been interchangeably tucked into the Book of the Bread of Life instead of into the book of daily bread. Memory pictures Grandmother rocking gently in her high-backed chair while fragrant loaves or biscuits bake; her feet are on the hassock, her spectacles down to her nostrils; the midmorning sunshine is streaming in through ruffled curtains over the red geraniums in her window boxes; her Bible is on her lap. Grandmother's Bible did not dwell on the wrath of God, and chapters with un-Victorian frankness were to her as though they had never been. To her the Bible was a Book of Comfort, not of Judgment.

Grandmother's Bible stayed wholesome. It had a more mellow effect on character than Grandfather's. The strength of spirit which her Bible gave her was not dependent on scholastic certification. The Twenty-Third Psalm was true to her heart, whether David wrote it or some later Levite. What did she care for historicity when she read Isaiah 35 and 53, Luke 15, John 6, 14, and 17, I Corinthians 13, Romans 8, and Revelation 21? The holiness of such chapters was and is unassailable. For *holiness is in proportion to verifiability in our own higher experience.*

Grandmother took her Bible as God's word, yes. Yet in practice the frayed edges of her familiar pages marked her sources of peace, canonized by the comfort they imparted. With no cloying insipidity her children's children might well know that Bible within the Bible. It is not necessary to thread all the maze of its genealogies, its history and exegesis, to possess or be possessed by *this* selected Scripture.

Yet to both Grandfather and Grandmother the same doctrine of literal inspiration was inherent. The Bible was unique among all the other books in the world, not merely in degree but in kind. It was magic. They took the King James Bible as they found it, and they never doubted that it had been dictated to the amanuenses of the Holy Spirit, verbatim to commas and i-dottings. No slightest echo of the Higher Criticism had unsettled their estimate. The Bible was the stable axis of their living.

Both Grandmother's and Grandfather's Bibles have pretty much vanished. Except for fundamentalists, regard for them seems to be swirling into the reverse of disregard. What is the actual status of the Scriptures these days?

That the Bible is still the world's best seller indicates nothing definite. This is no barometer of actual valuation. The Bible Societies' statistics of distribution and the Gideons' supplying of hotel rooms prove little of the Bible's vital influence or intelligent appreciation. The Bible is the Classic of classics. But we are reminded that a classic is a book we think we know all about, never having read it. Under the pressure of the practicalities and by the separation of church and state in education, even as an item of liberal culture it may be more honored in the breach than in the observance. Shakespeare and Caeser have more chance of a bowing acquaintance than St. John or Job. The mistaken halo of sanctity around the Old and New Testaments has been their handicap.

Proofs of contemporary ignorance are abundant. Allusions to scriptual characters or the quotation of great sentences are met with a blank stare. All four of the Information Please experts fell down on the question, "What is meant by Abraham's Bosom?" In a test of four thousand college youths only 30 per cent could name six people who knew Jesus; fewer yet could give five events in his life. "The Flood" was a typical answer. One-third rightly guessed that the Golden Rule was his most important teaching, but two thirds attempted no answer. Only 20 per cent would hazard any hint why the Church exists. One of Stanley Jones's mission teams polled the women leaders in fourteen major cities across the country, inquiring how many of them gave any definite place to the Bible in their home life; among these closely affiliated women of the churches the testimony tapered from 15 per cent to below five. Dr. Fosdick pillories the parsons themselves, writing:

"To more ministers than one likes to think, the use of the Bible is a difficult enigma. All the King's horses and all the King's men could hardly drag them into dealing with certain passages that used to be the glory of our fathers' preaching. . . . Still other preachers cut the Gordian knot by practically surrendering the Bible, save as by courtesy they use it in some oblique and cursory fashion to point a moral and adorn a tale."[1]

Rote Bible study should not be revived, even if it *could* be. There is no value in plowing straight through from Genesis

---

[1]Harry Emerson Fosdick, *The Modern Use of the Bible* (New York, 1924), p. 4.

1:1 to Revelation 22 under the whiplash of piety. The Bible has the right to fight for recognition of its ever-so-human processes. It would gain by being set into its own niche in the midst of other great literature. Its vindication can come only when it has ceased to have the false magical glamor of literal inspiration, by some knowledge of the psychology of the authors, their day's ideas of the divine and its dealings with human events and duties, and the modifications of original documents by biased second and third editorial redactors. In our tumultuous, utilitarian generation can there be hope of this except among scholars?

Certainly not, among the believers in a magic Bible. We are due for a new burst of Bibliolatry among those who seek some storm-cellar authority in a world which is too much for them. Grandfather's Bible has been moved out of the front parlor into that storm cellar in which fundamentalists of many sorts and kinds find strange comradeship.

The advocates of Biblical inerrancy in every word are all there, followers of the incredible radio programs of the Voice of Prophecy, the Foursquare Gospel, Jehovah's Witnesses, and Pentecostal Disciples. These are on one extreme; Billy Graham and other millennial revivalists are a bit nearer the center; Roman Catholic and neo-Catholic sacramentalists are over on the other extreme. The adherents of Karl Barth's "Wholly Other" God and Neo-Orthodoxy are near akin. Each of these rival groups has its own Bible within the Bible. They are like the priests of the Dark Ages who carried the key to the padlock on the lectern Bible and unlocked it to read what they chose, then locked it again. The fanatics choose their Key to the Scripture from Daniel, Revelation, and Matthew 22, and they argue their auguries with pet texts and a private vocabulary of First, Second, and Third Raptures of the Day of the Lord, which make the unconverted shrug their shoulders in disgust.

Reliance on the saving blood of Jesus too hideously duplicates trust in the human sacrifices on barbaric altars. A radio sermon on a national hookup, for example, said: "Judas's thirty pieces of silver at 4 per cent interest would fill 345 globes the size of the earth. Our sins compound the same way. But Christ died on the cross to pay the whole price we owe. He settled our account. Therefore God can now forgive us." Karl Barth himself, Sir Oracle to too many men in good theological schools and pulpits along with Kierkegaard, stakes his massive case for the "Wholly Other" God on special pleadings. And Rome has its own cornerstone test, "Thou art Peter."

How difficult it is to get an airplane view of the whole Biblical terrain. Few attempt it. It is much simpler to follow old General Booth's advice to theorists and Bible readers to treat bothersome or contradictory passages as he treated the bones of his breakfast bloater, putting them quietly on one side, and eating only the good meat. Any modern Tom Paine or Ingersoll could make fundamentalists squirm (if they would listen) by asking them how they condone Abraham's polygamy, Joshua's obedient sun, David's liquidation of his several Lidices, Solomon's lusts, Jonah's great fish, Mary's other children, Peter's coin-carrying fish, and the resemblance of Jehovah's hell to an nth-degree Buchenwald. A good revivalist who was blasting this author for his unsettling heresies boasted, "I have a closet in the back of my mind. When I am faced with a difficulty which I know would trouble me if I let it, I wrap it up, tie it tight, seal the knots, put it on the high shelf in the closet, lock the door, throw away the key and forget where I threw it. The name of that closet is *faith*."

Resistance against the encroaching tide of modern know-ledge is pathetic. Can we put ourselves inside the mind of such a man as Mr. Voliva in his project to sail a ship to the edge of the world and prove it is flat? Can we imagine the logic of Bible-belt campaigners to force their legislators to forbid the teaching of evolution in state universities? Darwin, Ingersoll, Clarence Darrow, Bertrand Russell, and their kind are still the straw men at which the Knights of the White Plume tilt, clad in the impenetrable armor of dogma. They do not realize that what they blast as anti-religious has much the same effect for the ultra-Protestants as the Catholic *Index Expurgatorius* has for Romanists: suspicion is only the more aroused and curiosity the more stimulated by the advertising.

Strangely enough, the King James Bible has become *the* Bible for the pious. It seems to have its own aura of oracular inerrancy. Modern translations are viewed with alarm by the ultra-traditionalists. Witness the fury of the hardshells at the audacity of the translators of the new Revised Standard Version who dared to go back to the Hebrew original to find out what Isaiah said of Emmanuel's mother and report back that he did *not* say "a virgin shall conceive" but "a young woman." "The whole doctrine of the virgin birth is defied!" cry the intransigents! They remind us of the mythical Granny who is supposed to have murmured, "If the King James Version was good enough for dear St. Paul, it's good enough for me."

Did the guardians of the authorized Book ever read through its own preface? Dedicating it to "that learned and judicious Prince" (who was no such), the scholars of that translation dared "the censures of ill-meaning and discontented persons whose calumniations and hard interpretations" would be fired by its modernity.

The defenders of the faith would find nothing absurd in the opening paragraph of a certain "Apology for the Bible," bound in cedar shingles and dated 1796, written by a horrified Lord Bishop against the author of the *Age of Reason:*

"I owe a duty to society to trouble you and the world with some observations on so extraordinary a performance. I hope there is no want of charity in saying that it would have been fortunate for the Christian world had your life been terminated before you had fulfilled your intention. In accomplishing your purpose you will have unsettled the faith of thousands; rooted from the minds of the unhappy virtuous all their comfortable assurance of a future recompense; will have annihilated in the minds of the flagitious all their fears of future punishment."

Tom Paine must have chortled over these phrases. But his pin-prickings were as nothing in comparison with the overhauling to which conscientious scholars now subject Holy Writ for its own good sake.

Grandmother's Bible was the Book of Comfort. It was her evangel. Its sentiments were not sentimentality. But can the evangelicals now in our midst parry the query whether their Bible is not sentimental?

Sentimentality is an escapism. It is a semi-magic, self-administered; for it omits the soul's labor. It gives emotional efflatus by spiritual thievery, which is possession without earning.

The Bible can be and often is profaned by those who pull out the tremolo stop about the "faith they learned at Mother's knee." They turn it into vapidly sweet hymns "written in the days when damsels wore ringlets and stays and hoopskirts and played the harp and swooned," and sung by mellifluous crooners. The man who sanctimoniously quotes platitudes may be consigning a liberal opponent to perdition. Religiosity is a conditioned reflex, unconscious cant. The Bible can be an arsenal of proof texts, and bigotry arms itself with them. Scripture can be prostituted. *And is!*

Both Grandfather and Grandmother got something out of their Bibles which was down below their surface. Grandfather was guided by a strict conscience. He was honorable, faithful, modest, and useful. However much his caliber was based on Old Testament ideals and however we may regret that the preaching to which he listened did not catch from the Master his flexible good will and charm, we must confess that if we lose the sturdiness of the prophets and the fire of Jesus, our fiber will be weak. To Grandfather the Persons of the Bible were pungently alive and ever-present. To Grandmother also, they were a very close, authentic company. They had issued forth from the pages of the Book into stimulating companionship.

Great gains have been made in our generation in the freeing of the original Persons of the Bible from the manipulations of exploiters and theorists. Scholarship had dug deep. If we care to, we can stand nearer to the heroes today than anyone has stood since they were in the flesh. Jesus of Nazareth, in particular, has been divested of subsequent legend and is once again the Son of Man, speaking with the genius which he uniquely had, to those who will listen. The methodology by which the experts have separated the wheat *of* him from the chaff *about* him may be too intricate for busy laymen; nevertheless they can take the results of this meticulous study on faith in the experts' skill and honor.

For example, we may easily gain some smattering of their

conclusions about the Gospels. It is intelligent to know that Mark's story probably embodies the memories of Peter; that Matthew includes an original edition which was the compilation of the sayings of Jesus, which may be of verbatim jottings by the disciple himself; and that a later compiler wove the Sayings into the story by Mark, together with much later legends of the birth and resurrection, which Mark did not know. It is reassuring that Luke was evidently the trained literary ex-slave of some Greek aristocrat converted by Paul who gave Luke to Paul as traveling comrade and amanuensis; and that during Paul's two years in prison Luke used the time to collect all the witness and growing legend of Jesus he could glean in Palestine, using Mark and the Sayings as his skeleton outline. Read the first four verses of his story to see how he felt about the existent materials. It is well to know that the so-called Gospel of John, although there runs through its fabric the thread of an unquestionable firsthand witness, is a Greek philosophizing of a Christ who is more mystically Stoic than Galilean, and that its special beauty of thought and language is of the Christianity which is perhaps a century after Paul. It is fair for us to guess what formative tendencies were building and coloring the oral tradition before the Gospels were written, and were in the vast wave of apocryphal gospels which further magicized Jesus. It is good to know such things, but not necessarily in detail. Jesus himself has once more been presented to us for the taking. So likewise have the other greatest figures of this Book, which is made up of such variant books—best, good, muddled, or useless. The hard-headed publishing trade knows its market. There have never been so many books of religious exposition as there are now. Any new book list proves that we are out of the doldrums into the *start* of intelligent Biblical interest. No one can complain that Biblical realities are unobtainable or withheld—unless he is under the thumb of a censor.

The false Bible is outmoded. Its defense is frenzied in proportion as its defenders feel the brunt of the attack on it by realism. The true Bible gives us the record of the great-hearts of the Hebrew genius and their successive spiritual discoveries. The ultimate authenticity of their record is in the contagion of Persons to persons. The real Persons of the Bible are forever relevant. The prophets are now what they were, majestic critics of all misguided religiosity and of brutal materialism. They were gifted with such moral insight as refutes any reputation for mere magic soothsaying. They were the conscience of their race, insisting that religion must be *religious,* and that nothing short of personal experience of the divine will suffice. The Son of Man towers head and shoulders above them, pertinent and arresting and greatly, greatly human. Again he lifts his voice to call across our tortured world: "He that hath ears to hear, let him hear."

Surely the issue of issues is of realistic religion. No other counts. We of this moment could lift human relations a notch higher if we unitedly would. Not to know the objectives is tragically inept. Is our vagueness about the objectives related to the haunting wonder whether they represent anything real? Are we well into Armageddon without knowing it?

We must have all the contagious inspiration from greatness we can get—from those who have met essentially the same enemies and stood against their assault. They are comrades in the noble battle to make the ideal real and actual. If we but knew it, they, with the great ones from all other Scriptures, can be our running start. There is no meaning in history unless it is that ideals have authority of the Spirit above the squabblings and blunderings of fools.

We cannot do God's will unless we know it. We cannot know it unless we are willing to learn it. *We cannot learn it better than by experience with those who demonstrate it.* The Word has indeed become flesh and dwells among us. It comes to its own. Do its own receive it or not?

CHAPTER ELEVEN

The Son of Man

However realistic, however modern, however humanistic religion may be, the personality and teaching of Jesus of Nazareth are inescapably to be reckoned with. Other giants of spiritual genius must also be accorded their full measure of gratitude; our appreciation of the central hero of the culture in which we have our roots should not blind us to the strength and beauty of other heroes. We are the children of a culture which fuses Christianity with Western ideas; we have the prophets and Jesus side by side with Socrates, Plato, Euripides, and Zeno the Stoic. Yet to most of us who know anything of his human magnificence, Jesus is naturally the one through whom we make our approach to inspiration most directly. He is our "first among equals."

He would not care how we ranked him over against others. He parried haloed pre-eminence with, "Why callest thou me good? There is only One who is good—that is, God." For whatever help he could be, by telling and living what life meant to him, he hoped to be a seed that falls into the ground of others' minds and hearts and dies to self, to give the earth where it falls the power to express *itself* in the new plant, made of that earth.

His use of the name "Son of Man" should be disinterred from beneath subsequent tradition and misunderstanding. In the original Hebrew usage "Son of Man" meant typical Man or Everyman, a human who epitomized humanness. Jesus never truckled with that artificial meaning of supernatural transcendence which later generations spoiled with Messianic implications of Apocalyptic melodrama. He kept the name modest and relevant to human norms, as though to assert that divinity is not oil in the water of human nature but rather the birthright of every son and daughter of man, revealed in any completely natural and loving life. Every human being is called to Messianic saviorhood. A Son of Man is a Son of God by birth into the life which is of the divine potence. He is "called" to bring the divine to bear on existence. He is "anointed" to this privilege.

It was not merely for the expedient reason that he would have been liquidated on the spot that he did not call himself Messiah. He cared so little what title he was given by the people because he cared so profoundly that they should have ears to hear his personal faith for what it might be worth to them by thoughtful assimilation into their own lives. He would not have used that title because what he meant by saviorhood was so diametrically the opposite of every current meaning for it that he would have been misunderstood as a blasphemer. His complete modesty prevented his use of such a name.

The next thing to note is that in public he carefully and always spoke of the Son of Man objectively—in the third person. He did not say, ever, "I am the Son of Man"; he said, "When the Son of Man cometh . . ." or "The Son of Man is Lord even of the Sabbath." Only at the very last when the crucifixion would demonstrate to the utmost that there could be no claim of supernaturalism did he vouchsafe "Thou sayest" to the name Caiaphas had evidently learned from Iscariot.

Jesus thought and taught that every individual is uniquely the recipient of God's self-imparting gift of life, exactly as

a good mother calls each of her children dearest. He would
have loved the bit in Thornton Wilder's homely play *Our
Town,* which tells of "that letter Jane Crofut got from her
minister when she was sick. On the envelope the address
was like this; it said, 'Jane Crofut, the Crofut Farm, Grover's
Corners, Sutton County, New Hampshire, United States of
America, Western Hemisphere, the Earth, the Solar System,
the Universe, the Mind of God.' "[1] So in his or her own
personal importance, everyone should know himself or herself.

No thoughtful analyst misses Jesus' intuition that human
existence is permeated by that which for want of a better
name we call the divine. Evolution is explained by its *élan
vital.* Existence is refined into grace and fellowship by its
magnetism. If we may rescue a superb term from its
churchy associations and give it a Humanist-plus content, we
can say that Jesus' thesis was of incarnation, the faith that the
divine is the human and the human is essentially the divine.
Jesus was working to fulfill this in himself and others. For
their sake he developed his own incarnation.

Every revealer of our common possibilities lifts our own
standards higher and stirs us to share his high experience.
Once they are lived out in our experience, the Galilean's
truths are inescapably contagious. Jesus expressed surprise
that others did not always feel the "of course" of the axioms
by which he spontaneously acted. He felt no pride because
he happened to know them, but he found his joy in being
like a clear pane of glass through which the sunlight of
reality might shine into the lives he loved.

It is strange that the central premise of Jesus' certainties
has been so overlaid and smothered by those people who have

---

[1]Thornton Wilder, *Our Town* (New York, 1938), Act I, p. 54.

used him as stalking horse for their own impossible magic theories, until it is hard to state this premise clearly and simply enough to make it rational and scientifically real. Yet it is so wholehearted and so consistent, once it is clear! Jesus acted on the conviction that one's personal life is not contained inside himself, insulated from other self-contained lives, but that one's personal life radiates itself from the personal center, with the range into which its forthgiving good will projects it.

Personal life is outgoing, self-imparting to others, in dynamic and qualitative gift of self. It is forthgiving in proportion to the intensity of one's compassion, of one's unselfish caring. It is life-transfusion.

The naive faith of the centurion, Jesus said, was greater than any he had found in all Israel. "I am a man under authority [i.e., I am the extension of authority], having soldiers under me [who are my self-extension], and I say to this one Go, and he goeth, and to another Come, and he cometh, and to my servant, Do this, and he doeth it. Speak thy word only [a self-extension] and my servant shall be healed." That is, he believed in the gift of self which Jesus' personality could accomplish. Such self-radiating love can be so deep a caring that it identifies the life of the giver with the life of the recipient of its strength. Furthermore, sympathy somehow gladly draws out of the loved life something of its pain or wrong, as a friend puts his lips to a snake bite and sucks out the poison which would kill his comrade. The only sin is selfishness, the life-miser's refusal to care and to give himself, or, even worse, the vampirism which drains life from others to glut its own. He who saves (hoards) his life loses real living. He encysts himself. Reciprocal life-giving survives all the deaths to selfish selfhood and gives to mutuality so new a richness that it proves its increase of divineness by results.

To snatch from ecclesiastical dogmatics their second magicized term, atonement—only, to rehabilitate it, shall we say *at-one-ment?* Jesus called it Christhood. It is a give and take saviorhood. The Golden Rule is its key. The Sermon on the Mount is the Son of Man's philosophy. The Beatitudes show his happiness in daily Christliness.

Blessed are the unspoiled
Blessed are the redemptive.
Blessed are the teachable.
Blessed are those who are in earnest about goodness, beauty and truth.
Blessed are those who *do* mercy.
Blessed are those who are completely idealistic.
Blessed are life-imparters.
Blessed are those who are glad, if need be, to suffer for their ideals.

In what other rationale can we link the parables of the Prodigal Son, the Good Samaritan, the Good Shepherd, the Leaven, the Sower's Seed and the Soils, the Salt of the Earth and the Bread of Life? In several of these he unforgettably scores the self-centered, life-greedy in their spider webs of rapacity or in parasitism. The elder brother of the Prodigal is emphasized in that parable which he cast in the teeth of the infallibilists who called Jesus a sinner. Imagine the irony of that graphic parable of the boastful Pharisee in the Temple who stood over against the needy publican and proudly prayed "with himself." What pungent stories they are: the vineyard workers who haggled for their penny a day and thus cheated themselves of the master's generosity; the ignominious poltroon who wrapped his talent in a nap-

kin and buried it; the smug snobs in the Parable of the
Last Judgment (it *is* only a parable) who had never given
a cup of cold water to the thirsty or shown any other humanness; the rich man who disdained the beggar at his door
and awoke to self-condemnation too late; the priest and the
Levite tiptoeing past the highwayman's victim on the
Jericho Road!

Notice that in the report of every healing "miracle" Jesus
expressly shows that his concern was with the fundamental
need of the sufferer, which was his life at the core. He said
to the man let down through the roof, "Son, thy sins be put
away." To the woman who touched his garment, he said,
"O Woman, great is thy faith; be it done unto thee in ac-
cordance with it." For he saw that "virtue" had been drawn
out of his life by her need. He asked another, 'Have you
enough will to be healed?"

But it is a commentary on the appetite for magic that the
Gospelers never accounted as miracles such transformations
of character as Zaccheus' or Simon Peter's or Levi Matthew's,
where there was no physical ill. Yet it was the same spirit
always at work.

In the chapter on Christian Science the distinction was
stressed between organic and functional troubles. Every
healing reported and played up in the *earliest* Gospel-records
seems to have been functional. There are implied explanations in the stories—as of the raising of Jairus' daughter, of
whom Jesus bluntly said she was not dead but sleeping (i.e.,
in coma). Where there is spirit to which spirit may give
itself and where organic ailments are not involved, there may
be a basic fact for the tale which the later magic stories mis-
construed.

However, when we come to the nature miracles, we must say flatly and at once that they are completely impossible. They are against the whole idea of the Son of Man, as well as against all natural law. That coin in the fish's mouth to pay the head tax, the multiplication of the loaves and the fishes, the water turned into wine, the blasted fig tree, the walking on water, the physical resurrection—these are repugnant to reason. And the pity of it is that these crude tales of necromancy hid the beauty and meaning of what presumably were the real events. The feeding of the multitudes was an acted parable, with the elder brother of this great family of faith adapting its well-known ceremony of broken bread into a communion symbolism of self-giving, enough and to spare. The water turned into wine hints a lost parable of the change from insipid existence into zestful life by the marriage of the divine bridegroom and the human soul. Certainly all the miracles of the Fourth Gospel, which had so long a time to grow into stories of legerdemain, still have remnants of the teachings which may have been the germ of their later legend.

Jesus taught a doctrine of saviorhood which was the role of everyone, but he gave it no name. Least of all did he openly claim his own savior privilege. As has been mentioned, if he had called that privilege Messianic, the utter opposite of his meaning would have been inferred. However, when he came to the moment when hostile officialdom was poised for the kill, he tested the Twelve to find if they had at all caught the clue of his concept. His question, "Whom say men that I am?" evoked an answer which showed that no one anywhere had guessed his meaning. "Some say John the Baptist, some Elijah, others Jeremiah, or some, one of the prophets." "But whom say ye that I am?" then brings Peter's impulsive answer, "Thou art the Christ, the Son of the Blessed." Allowing for later sharpening of that answer, Peter meant more than mere identification. His reply meant that out of comradeship with a Galilean carpenter they had come to a dawning new ideal of the divinity a humble human life can hold. Jesus' exclamation, "Thou art Peter and on this rock I will build my church," follows this up with a reply which holds a significance totally other than the exploiting one read into it by Rome. Jesus was making a serious play on words. *Peter* is a nickname for a stone—a piece of rock. Jesus had refused ever to use Simon's own name, for the Simon he first knew was as unreliable as quicksilver. This standardizing nickname Jesus had repeated and repeated, impressing Simon with his confidence that he could become stable and reliable. "On this rock"—a piece of stone; Peter would be a sample of all the Simons that would be made into "Peters" by comradeship with a savior. And lastly, the word translated *church* did not mean an institutional organization; "ecclesia" is the name for the Greek town meeting in which freemen united in the faith that an over-mind would speak through the fellowship. It is in the pattern of Jesus' informal friendship that he thought forward to a fellowship of free comrades in a shared birthright. Whatever he actually said in the vernacular Aramaic gave *that* concept its momentum. But what ecclesiasticism has made of *ecclesia!*

The final events of this young man's drama have suffered deeply from pious tradition. Palm Sunday has been caricatured as a triumphal entry into Jerusalem. It was not. It was Jesus' demonstration that the idea of a magic Messianic victory was without any foundation. The mob did not acclaim *him* as Messiah, but as "He that should come," the human preparer for the celestial Messiah's descent out of the clouds.[2] The mob was swept by the hysteric delusion that when this forerunner crossed the threshold of the Temple, the crack of doom would sound and the end of the age come to pass. Jesus was calmly aware that they must be disillusioned. He mounted an ass instead of a warhorse; he made no response to the palm-waving and the hosannas ("Blessed is *he that cometh in the name of the Lord*"). Tears came to his eyes at their misguidedness but he carried through the scene to destroy their false hopes. There was a progressive anticlimax. The theatric dream of a magic denouement was deflated, the yelling died, the country folk fell away, Jerusalem loomed impregnable, and when Jesus entered the Temple court heaven was decisively silent. He and the baffled disciples were all that remained of the processional; as he had foreseen, the crowds, their hysteric anticipation destroyed, melted away. Now the cautious officials could safely crucify him.

Neither has the treachery of Judas been understood by traditionalists. His thirty pieces of silver, the standard price of a slave such as only a freeman could sell, signified the bargain that freed Judas from the penalties of association with the insurrectionist Jesus was accused of being. These coins were not given Judas merely to lead the squad of soldiers to arrest Jesus. It was something more vital. Judas sold what he thought to be Jesus' secret belief about himself as Messiah, a claim easily distorted as blasphemy. To the widely asked question "Whom does this man believe himself to be?" Judas answered "Messiah." The high priest, Caiaphas, with

---

[2]See Albert Schweitzer, *The Mystery of the Kingdom of God* (New York, 1914), pp. 156-163.

no understanding of Jesus' connotation and no desire to understand except in the conventional way, could twist the charge of supernaturalist presumption into that name and judge Jesus deserving of death according to the law. Judas had given Caiaphas the excuse to discredit and kill this madman amidst acclaim from the Passover populace whose reactions the officials had hitherto feared. When the Sanhedrin met, Caiaphas dramatized histrionically, rending the carefully provided rending-strip of his pontifical vestment, crying loudly, "Behold, now we have heard his blasphemy, what think ye." No wonder he got the answer, "He is guilty of death!"

Jesus had foreseen the cross. He had cut straight across the authority of the Pharisiac law; he had touched the Sadducees' pocketbook nerve about their Temple abattoir for sacrifices, and had been at the center of disturbances easily construed to Pilate as threatening the Pax Romana. He knew the fate of those who did this. For when only a twelve-year-old boy he had seen Judas of Gamala's rebels nailed up at every crossroad in Galilee. It was the execution reserved by Rome for its worst criminals. Nevertheless, Jesus was unshakenly certain that even crucifixion could not kill his living spirit. His enemies might have his body; they could not touch *him*.

All martyrdom for a cause is more than a physical death. Ideals are only abstract hypotheses until they are lived out. Jesus was so sure that his ideals would spread and grow, and his life, so lost, would find the heaven of the human heart, that he could promise with certainty, "Where two or three are gathered together in my name, there am I in their midst."

Give Jesus the credit of magnificent consistency. Both Gethsemane and Golgotha were victorious by this faith. It

is outrageous that the Church has slavered them with pity.
The report of Gethsemane has been steadily traduced as his
struggle to avoid the cross. Nothing could be more unjust.
To begin with, who saw what occurred in that garden? No
one was with him. The breathless lad (John Mark?) who
had been roused by the tramp of the guard, and had run
crosslots to warn Jesus, might have climbed onto the wall,
seen the Master in the moonlight, and may have heard a
phrase of his prayer that the "cup" might pass from him.
What cup? Naturally, the cup of loathing for the ignominy
and barbarity ahead. He was bracing himself *for* death.
After all the unflinching resolution in anticipation of the
end, it is unthinkable that he quailed at last and whimpered
to escape it. He could have escaped, even then, by groveling
before his overlords and pleading pardon for his "lunacy."
But no; he wrestled to overcome the horror of the obscene
death ahead; *and he won*. The cup had passed.

And every one of the sentences from the cross was confident and exalted—especially the most cruelly slandered sentence of his whole life, which was instead utterly confident
and daring! Only people without rudimentary objectivity
toward the Bible could interpret it as a wail of dispair. *"Eloi,
Eloi, Lama Sabachthani!"* The pulpits of churches are wet
with tears of pity for him who in his last hour cried that
"God had forsaken him," but they have failed to consider
the Twenty-Second Psalm. Those words, cried "in a loud
voice," were not uttered in vernacular Aramaic but in Hebrew. It was the beginning of the synagogue's psalm in its
ritual tongue, as Jesus had learned it; and as he spoke, it was
the *whole* psalm that he had in his mind. The psalm says
that seemings are *not* realities: the seeming of the moment
is forsakeness, abysmal desertion by God; but the reality is

that God has *not* forsaken his own, that he has *not* hidden his face from his own; that "the meek shall be satisfied and all the ends of the earth shall remember and turn unto the Lord; a seed shall serve Him; they shall come and declare His righteousness unto a people that shall be born," for "his heart shall live forever." When Jesus lifted his voice to cry out this psalm with all his mind and soul and strength, the strength which failed his body did not fail his victorious spirit.

"Father, into Thy hands I commit my spirit." This was the "Now I lay me" of every Jewish child, unafraid of the gentle dark and happy in the certainty of a new day beyond the night. So Jesus committed his spirit, which was and is his *life,* to the workings of the divine, and thus to the heaven which is within us. Within *us?*

CHAPTER TWELVE

Prayer? Worship? Sacraments?

PRAYER

Skepticism about prayer, or rather, about prayers, is perhaps more prevalent than is skepticism about any other religious project. And this skepticism is rife because the too usual forms are overloaded with misconceptions. They seem ignoble to mature minds. The vestigial ideas inside the old forms insult both divinity and humanity. As petitionary lobbying to a Santa Claus deity, their sanctified selfishness is too petty to endure. Men and women with self-respect are repelled by candle-burning and rosary rote, by the copyrighting use of Jesus' name, and by the patter of the Lord's Prayer as an Open Sesame. Luck insurance is outmoded. Prayer-magic has been discarded because man's decencies have driven him toward a more effective life act. It is because there is in him a possibly unformulated but better faith that he recoils from notions which stultify its urge.

Jesus is on the side of this emergent faith. He spoke sternly when he said, "Use not vain [empty] repetitions as the heathen do, for they imagine they will be heard for their much babbling; after this fashion [of soul] pray ye. . . ." It is not the words but the train of thought and the conditioning of will which he means. Ritual abracadabras are profanity worse than cursing, for the ideology which shapes these incantations is void of true comprehension of the God who is Life.

"My prayers are not answered," whimpers some disappointed wheedler for favors. He shows his conception of prayer as either a labor-saving device or a panhandling hope of a deity-bountiful. He has not faced up to the fact that desired results have to be wrought out by one's own effort as far as it can be carried. One's own effort gives the chance for the larger Life to mesh into the actualities, just as the wiring between the dynamo and the light bulb in our room provides the connection for the electricity. The lamentation that prayers remain unanswered betrays the fact that blessings have been sought rather than the touch of God flooding into the co-operative will and soul. Specific blessings may or may not eventuate from the fresh strength of the energized person, but *if* they come they are only by-products of the vitalization.

The grip of such pathetic theories is obsessive. Here is a wartime dispatch as example:

> Contrary to common belief, General——was a deeply religious man. Before he turned his army north to rip Rundstedt's counter-offensive, he prayed for good weather for his Thunderbolts. He ordered his chaplain to print 250,000 Christmas greetings, on the back of which was a prayer for clear skies. They were distributed to his troops. As the counter-attack got under way, the clouds disappeared and a break in the weather brought five days of clear, sunshiny skies. During those five days the army's Thunderbolts had a field day, blasting the enemy's tanks and columns as they retreated. The General telephoned his chaplain, "Print another 100,000 of those prayers."[1]

What an exposé of credulity and crudity! It was pure accident that it didn't rain. Suppose it had poured. Did the

---

[1] *Time*, Vol. 45, No. 5, Jan. 29, 1945, p. 88; see also *Newsweek*, same date.

general think that the Eternal would take sides and manipulate the elements so that he could slaughter hecatombs of Germans who had no such inside track with deity? And did the chaplain have the same belief?

No sincere prayer is ever unanswered. It gets the reciprocal flow of the more-than-individual overlife. Real praying is like breathing—instinctive and imperative. By his own action the breather draws in air, the oxygen cleanses his blood, he exhales his poisons, and his energy is heightened. And breathing is the constant interplay of the whole atmosphere and the participating individual. By the oxygen of the Infinite he lives and moves and has his renewed being. Prayer is a two-way act.

Three suggestions follow as to the rationale of that prayer which is of the spirit underneath any wordings or wordlessness.

(1) Normal people go on the principle that existence can be bettered, and that if it can be it should be. Pessimists sneer that the theory of progress is not borne out by the record of history or of personal character. Yet the pessimists are judging existence a failure by the standard of what they feel it ought to be but isn't. They and we both hate the gloomy decision that existence is a squirrel cage in which there is no advance. And we hate that gloomy theory because we feel in us the instinct of the future. We insist that there are objectives and that our dreams and ideals are incentives toward possibilities to be realized. Like the small girl struggling with the buttons down the back of her dress who explained, "You see, I'm in front of myself," we face front not only with mouth, ears, nose, hands, and feet but with emotions, will, mind, and some sort of faith. We are stabbed by divine dis-

content with the present as a finality. We are stirred to make actuality come up to the ideal. Real praying is the operation of vital intuition and resolution. When we are laid hold of by the future our prayer for its fulfillment is already begun.

(2) There are energies in which our forward reach by the spirit finds that strength. We are carried on by the stream of life once we launch ourselves into it. We can deliberately put ourselves into its current and rely on it to sweep us in its steady flow; we will then find our hopes and resolution and our labor caught by its unflagging flood.

This lifts us up out of selfish individualism. As the greater interest is gained, the more faithful is our partnership in it. If our passions are centripetal, pulling forever toward a personal center, there can be no sharing in the centrifugal dynamic. But open-souled people will know the pulse of self-transcendence and will achieve selfless measure by it.

The true realist both uses and is borne up by the Creative Purpose which springs from its hidden source and courses down past all obstacles toward its destiny. In each mystic act there is self-losing and self-finding, and also a launching beyond self.

> "Ah, but a man's reach
> Must exceed his grasp!"

(3) Every true prayer is proleptic. Is proleptic too high-brow a word? It summarizes the whole transaction. For it means that standing where one now is, a man reaches forward to what can be, lays hold on it, and holding fast, pulls himself and is pulled out of what is, toward what can be.

Speaking in his vernacular Aramaic or perhaps in some sentence of synagogue Hebrew, Jesus used a word in the

Lord's Prayer which, although it is given to us as only "daily" bread, evidently had proleptic overtones. For the Greek translation, *epiousion,* indicates "bread for the morrow."[2] And, knowing Jesus' habit of mind which read into everyday practicalities a parabolic significance, we are probably licensed to connect the idea of the Bread of Life[3] and the Upper Room symbolism with this. At any rate, the prayer is for our portion of the day-by-day bread which gives continuing and forward-going strength. And if, according to his symbolic trait, this is to have allegorical connotation, why shouldn't we conjecture a deeper idea along with "bread for the morrow": "Give us day by day our portion of the Bread of Life, strengthening us to pass through any night into a greater tomorrow"?

Joan of Arc once cried "To build and build and build on running sands! How terrible it must be to be God!" But God is proleptic. He is ceaselessly "becoming."

There is a homely allegory in a "proleptic" invention by a one-time Grand Manan fisherman. The tides of Fundy must be respectfully reckoned with by those who go down to the sea in their cockleshell boats. It is disconcerting to be caught offshore if the wind dies and the swells grow oily and the gulls yammer and the boat rocks impotently and the dusk is falling. In the days before the fishermen had motors in their boats, a local inventer contrived what he called a harpoon anchor. To the backward points of a harpoon spearhead he hinged small anchor flukes and he tied a coil of thin, strong rope to the haft of the weapon. Then, when a boat was be-

----

[2] E.g. Moffat, Matthew 6:11—"Give us this day our bread for the morrow"; also in American Revised Version.

[3] In the Fourth Gospel (John 6), of course, but with derivation from earlier sources, probably.

calmed or a tide rip threatened, the strongest man of the crew would stand in the bow, heave this harpoon as far as he could, yank the flukes open when the spear struck bottom; and, if it caught, the crew would take hold and pull the boat forward the rope's length. Over and over the harpoon would fly ahead and take lodgment on the bottom, over and over again the crew would pull on the rope—and home they'd come at last. True prayer is a harpoon anchor. What more do we need to know of its process? It is a proleptic act of the will, the mind, the affections, the imagination, and the faith which commandeers us, all in one outreach.

Yet the allegory of the harpoon anchor is inadequate. For proleptic prayer is also pulled by the divine. Our prayer is as much a response to *its* prayer to us as ours is to it. Paul was phrasing evolution before its scientifically defined theory when he wrote, "The Spirit also helps our infirmities, for we know not what we should pray for as we should; but the Spirit itself makes intercession for us with groanings which cannot be uttered." (Endeavors or earnest struggle would be better wording.) If we feel this, we feel ourselves worth something in the life process.

There are credulous pray-ers, of course, who swear that miraculous answers have come to them. And there are countless others who persist even with hope deferred, whose faces shine with patient trust that their turn will yet come when God's will is their way.

That which comes to the life of the patient or gratified pray-er does not come from his articulated petitions; it comes subconsciously in quality of values because the unarticulated prayer, which is the true one, struggles through. That canny Scot, quoted elsewhere on "doubt," twinkled with wit as he also exclaimed, "The verra firrst thing God maun do

wi' oor prayers is t'poonctuate and make sense oot o' them."
Even a blundering, wrongly conceived, would-be intercession may channel a sincerity of spirit which, apart from the
mental error, may get through to touch by the vital Power.
The heart has truths of experience of which the shallow or
immature mind may be ignorant. What we want to discover is what happens to the *soul* for *its* good, down underneath even our best efforts at prayer. That is what affects
the tone and timbre of mutual living, by radiation from the
changed pray-er.

WORSHIP

Many more people stay away from church services than go
to them. Their disregard of worship points to some prevalent
reaction. Boredom, banality, pretense, offensive unrealism —
these are the reasons which are given. The scoffer says he
doesn't like vestments and sacraments, pulpiteering, long
prayers bringing the Lord up to date, and Gospel hymns.
He ascribes to the offices of the churches a platitudinous sentimentalism, pretentious melodrama, emotional nudism, mor-
bidity. His repugnance and indifference is shown toward
Catholic and semi-Catholic thaumaturgy, preacher-centered
adorations (or criticisms), Prayer Book "canned liturgy,"
fundamentalist Bible-quoting, and cultist fetishism.

The sneerers shut their minds to the good, which, for all
the abuses of it, is the explanation of worship's survival. Easy
scorn for the grotesque distortions of worship is not quite
discriminating. The cant and the arrogance of glib services
should be blasted as blasphemy with all the wrath they deserve; but, as with prayer, deep sincerity of effort can carry
a spirit the vocabulary does not define.

The idea of God has so far outgrown all primitive picturing that it has left a vacuum in the crowd's religious thinking. Dean Inge aptly mutters that most people take God as merely the head of the clerical profession. Though it was once called the queen of sciences, Theology is no longer rated as a science worthy of companionship with the other sciences. It hasn't the flavor of fact to the popular mind. Nothing definite seems to accrue from its process. Worship ought to be "worth-shape," but isn't. So its critics accuse.

There are two kinds of honesty. In a way it is honest to level our words down to what we happen to feel at the moment; it is a finer kind of honesty to level sincerity up to what we know we ought to feel. The lower honesty is a meat-axe bluntness. Suppose some visitor whom I don't want to see comes to my door. Meat-axe "frankness" would let me bar the threshold and growl, "You here! Sorry to see you. On your way!" But the ritual called courtesy compels me to say, "Glad to see you, man! Come in. And don't hurry off." That isn't all, though. The ritual of courtesy commands me to *make myself mean what I say*. There is no value in the formula itself; I can make it a hypocrisy. Or I can bring about a change in myself by deliberately lifting myself into meaning what I know I should both say *and feel*. Ritual and liturgy are under the same possibilities. If worship is free of formalism there are results to be had by the higher kind of honesty—provided the form is honest too.

The ideal Book of Worship should contain prayers, canticles, and psalms which are the skimmed-off cream of religious utterance, bequeathed to corporate worship through the centuries. All worship items, however, must be submitted to a ruthless overhauling in every generation, to perceptive expurgation and reshaping according to the new era's advancing philosophy. In typical worship there is a lot of embalmed medievalism and fundamentalism which should have no sanctity by association. The "forms of sound words" which have become a fixation may be a fine museum exhibit but their *mana* has evaporated. The great liturgies should be combed, altered, and enriched. No false reverence should halo them.

A certain inept parson was solemnly addressing the children of his church school. (This is an actual fact.) "Dear boys and girls, do you know what reverence is? Do you know the feeling you have when you go into a cemetery after dark? That is reverence. That is how you should feel when you come into church." Too many people do. And a liturgy which is mortuary is defunct. Small marvel it is that hard-headed utilitarians judge all myticism as fatuous fantasy and that they vilify culture and historic birthrights. The traditionalists who will fight to the death to keep a semicolon or a vacuous archaism only violate the soaring spirit of the original authors whose outgrown words voiced that which was more than their tongues could tell.

Worship is an art and great artists are scarce. It takes a combination of high realism and great emotion. The imponderables are essential, the holiness of beauty as well as the beauty of non-pious holiness, to lead to understanding and sane hope. The form of worship is a test, not only to the leader and composer of it, but to the worshiper even more. If it is a worship which can be entered into with utter honesty, its ideals accomplish much for the co-creator of its values. Entering into or, rather, carried along with jabberwocky magic, worshipers take no responsibility either for the "miracle of the altar" or for threshing out the wheat from the chaff of the pulpit exercises.

Some sentinel with a two-edged sword should quote to

every worshiper the arresting requirements of King Arthur's court:

> When ye pass beneath this archway . . .
> The King will bind you by such oaths
> As is a shame a man should not be bound by,
> But which no man can fully keep.

SERMON-TASTING

Listening to a sermon is not worship. The exalting of the sermon above worship is a confession that worship is too difficult for the capacity of the man in the pew. Is the sermon another magic? The temptation to the preacher is to focus on histrionics. He may be betrayed into actorial tricks, judging his output by applause for his magical oratory. The pulpit is often called Coward's Castle because the preacher allows no questioning of his "divine authority." But sermons which come from mental travail, with a touch of the agony that wrestling for truth must have, have something authentic to proffer.

This is no demurrer against honest sermons in their place. As specialists in the psychology of religion, in the history of religions, and in the moral problems of fellow men and women, ministers ought to have something constructive to give to their people. They are expected to study, to pray, to learn human traits by touch with the flock, to climb Sinai and meet God face to face, then return to tell what they have learned there. Be charitable toward men so held to revelation-on-order every week. Yet the best of them would say that worship is a more rigorous discipline than preaching — and potentially a greater blessing.

Is it too daring to suggest that the place for the sermon is therefore at the beginning of a service rather than at the end, where it appears to be the climax? The worship period is now generally thought of as a preliminary, to be scanted or exploited for the preaching to come, instead of the more ultimate act of the spirit, after initial conditioning. Yet Protestant custom has emphatically gone the way of sermon emphasis. Only when there are sacramental occasions is there the better chance.

SACRAMENTS

Sacraments are the moot problem. They are the most corrupted and prostituted ceremonies of the churches, though they should be the prime means to blessing. The two standard sacraments, of course, are baptism and the Lord's Supper (under whatever name). They are the cornerstone assets, but they are almost entirely falsified into magic. It is doubtful what church membership would be without these determinants. They give substance to ecclesiasticism. Yet their symbolism should be so simple and so natural that there would be no necessity for priestly or clerical monopoly over them. They should be the prerogative of the priesthood of all believers. Would that the meaning of these two sacraments were made evident to every wholesome man and woman as his own natural right. The dedication of children by dedicated parents has numberless sacramental rites and the breaking of bread by the family is a daily deed of shared life with all the overtones of a eucharist.

Baptism by the Church is insisted on by Catholics and orthodox Protestants alike. The Baptists rightly claim that the symbolism antedated Jesus, although they do not officially stretch that assertion to include other world religions, ancient and modern. The churches have co-opted the symbolism and denied the validity of all other baptisms — and often each other's. Baptism is "necessary to salvation," you know, "for-asmuch as our savior Christ saith, None can enter into the Kingdom of God except he be regenerate and born anew of water and the Holy Ghost." Vicious arguments are endless — whether immersion is obligatory or whether sprinkling will do, whether the Trinitarian formula is imperative as against the formulas which fail to mention Christ, whether there should be infant baptism or only adult, whether Protestant baptism is of any potence or only Catholic or Apostolic Successional.

We know how baptism has become too nominal. Parents bring their baby to the font in conformity to custom, perhaps still vaguely concerned to "give the child its name" and avoid the danger of limbo "if anything happens." They are still under the spell of the barbaric doctrine that unbaptized children will be kept out of heaven because the guilt of Adam is in them, making them heirs of damnation and children of wrath. They would see nothing but consistency in the tale of some missionary in the wilderness, captured by savages, who lures native youngsters close enough to his cage to reach out and swiftly make the sign of the cross on them with a finger-tip moistened in a drop of water in his cornhusks. These children are thereby made eligible for God's grace; otherwise not!

The whole tissue of prescribed method and sacerdotal copyright completely blots out John's and Jesus' meaning. John was called the Baptizer because he defied ecclesiastical monopoly in a way which ought not to be forgotten. He adapted the symbolism of baptism with sensational audacity. In his day it was a well-known ceremonial used only for two dramatic purposes. The first and standard one was for restoration to society after leprosy. Into the unspeakable horror of that loathsome disease the dogmatists had infused the insult that leprosy is always the punishment for heinous sin, known or unknown to the victim. If there were leprosy, that was evidence of God's punishment. The leper was unclean and contagious. If he were cured[4] he came to the priests to be baptized — that is, ceremonially washed and pronounced clean, fit for contact again because God had evidently been satisfied that the leper had sufficiently made expiation. The second use of baptism transferred the horror of leprosy's un-cleanness of body and soul to Gentilism, a leprosy just as re-volting and contaminating. If a Gentile wanted to be ac-cepted as a Jew, he disavowed his iniquitous Gentilism and was baptized.

John brazenly wrested this ceremonial symbolism from the institution's proprietorship and made it into his own arresting demand. He thundered that the worst leprosy of all is spiritual pride. He flung his ultimatum at the Pharisees, Scribes, and Sadducees, and against all who counted them-selves safe by their orthodoxy, crying out that they must ac-knowledge their leprosy of soul, repent and submit to the public humiliation of baptism. Furthermore, since life is organically a unity, each person who came to John's baptism did so not only in his individual capacity but as a repenting part of Israel. In this meaning, Jesus was baptized.

Now what becomes of the twisting of John's anti-ecclesi-astical symbolism? Present-day dogma falsifies John's idea when it is contended that Christ instituted the sacrament, without which salvation is impossible. So it is declared that baptism confers that which by nature we cannot have.

The Lord's Supper is perverted from its original spon-

---

[4]Eczema was then undifferentiated from leprosy. Hence there were possible cures.

taneity even more. It has become the magic-in-chief of all closed corporation churchianity. Perhaps it need not be re-iterated here how "Hoc est corpus" has dwindled to "Hocus pocus." The acted parable of the Upper Room has been betrayed.

Bread naturally suggests its own metaphoric interpreta-tion. Wheat grows by sunshine and rain from earth's re-sources; it is harvested, threshed, ground, and kneaded into dough to be baked, all by human labor. Thus both the divine and the human are in it. Wine is also the gift of the universe and the product of labor. Its sparkle and tang is for our joy. Bread and wine? Strength and joy, from God and human effort, together.

Bread has not fulfilled its purpose if it remains in a loaf or on a plate. It has fulfilled its reason for being only when it has been eaten, assimilated, and become strength in the eater. Wine has not fulfilled itself if it stays in a cup. It exists to tingle and glow in the blood.

At every high family meal the head of the oriental family took a loaf of bread and a cup of wine and blessed them — that is, *he declared them symbolic, which is all that a blessing does.* He broke the bread into fragments and distributed them; then he passed the cup. One loaf, one epitome of life, shared by all those who lived one intertwined life; one cup, one gift of zest in life, likewise shared.

Jesus stood at the head of the table the night before his death — the death he knew would come tomorrow. He was Elder Brother to this his disciple family. He enacted the familiar rite but he made it intensely personal with a new meaning. He was to die but he believed he was literally giv-ing his life to his friends. "Let this bread and this wine say my gift of self into your lives, with all the meaning you already ascribe to bread and wine now made personal — my life, as bread and wine, to be strength and zest in you. Whenever you break bread think of me in your midst." That's his sacrament. How informal and how moving and how real!

Although it is not claimed that they were instituted by Christ himself, there are five additional sacraments which the Catholic, Anglican, and Eastern Orthodox churches administer. These "mysteries" are confirmation, penance, extreme unction, holy orders, and matrimony. All of them are based on the magic idea of the Church as accredited by God and Christ to convey the Holy Spirit. The authority of the Church makes only those sacraments valid which are via Apostolic Succession, transmitting the grace of God.

The laying on of apostolic hands, the anointing with holy oil, the measuring out of the penance necessary before absolution, the ordination of clergy — these are all close corporation sacraments. And marriage, as a sacrament, is supposed to weld an indissoluble union between man and wife, once it is blest by the Church.

Popular understanding is that the marriage service is a sacrament (if there is one), for its vows, rings, and final blessing have all the earmarks of other sacramentally valid rites. How otherwise can "I pronounce you man and wife" be interpreted?

And, in addition, the tangle of marital decisions in trouble-cases seems to rest on something far more ecclesiastical than personally intimate. Sacerdotal policies are strangely insulated from the humanities. Since the usual estimate is that only 10 per cent of marriages can be called ideal, and 30 per cent are under dangerous strain or broken, the Church's rigid decisions are blind. The fact for which the churches have never made due allowance is that rebels against the sacramental standard are often the very persons who have highest, not the lowest ideals of marriage, whose longing for fulfillment is unquenchable even after disaster.

Until the churches admit that divorce for proven and deep-seated incompatibility can be a dignified step taken by decent and honest people, the churches will increasingly be by-passed by realists. Sacerdotalism is unsound in its obsession that there must be a guilty and an innocent party, and that it can extend its mercy only to the innocent.

In this shall we not be blunt enough also to say that civil law inherits from the churches the same demand that there must be a sinner over against each innocent? The courts go on the theory that the complainant must prove blameless and the defendant must be guilty of *something* — there must be the appearance of "sin."

The casuistries and dishonesties which the letter of the canon or the law causes are ignominious. The definitions of causes for annulment instead of divorce, the ridiculous criterion whether the partners "intended a true Christian marriage" when married, and, in the case of Rome, whether the original marriage was by a priest—these are hairsplittings.

The Church assumes that adultery is the one sin that voids marriage — but Jesus did not say so. The Church's business should be primarily of the spirit. The letter of the law is not. Here is one example of such canon-idolatry by the Church: A prominent woman, after twenty years of vain endeavor to salvage a marriage she had contracted far too young, found herself maturely in love with a fine-minded man. On either side of the existent marriage there was no violation of the marriage vow. Both husband and wife were decent people, but definitely incompatible. But her church denied her permission to remarry after divorce. Her husband, knowing how much her church meant to her, generously offered to provide her with the purely fictional appearance of unfaithfulness which would satisfy the letter of the church's rules. She was naturally unwilling that he should demean himself for her and went to her bishop to present the proposal of legal wiles, anticipating a severe rebuff. The bishop made answer that if the technicalities were met, he could give the necessary consent for remarriage! He was willing to make the church *particeps criminis* in collusion and legal fraud. To such a length must church and state go to provide the appearance of evil?

A new stubbornness of public opinion on behalf of marital truth is discernible. More and more, if the essence of a marriage has evaporated, divorce is preferred for its factual frankness. True marriage *is* advancing. Amid the dust of difficulties, the realities of marriage will more plainly emerge. Realism is beginning to win its present campaign against the pretension of magic authority for sacramentalist, inelastic, institutional rules.

No one lives without sacraments. The sin of ecclesiasticized sacramentalism is that it withdraws sacramental realization from our everyday companionships. The magical designation of its two cardinal rituals (and with some churches a peripheral five more) as the valid sacraments robs normal life of this meaningfulness. *The churches have cornered the sacrament market.* Yet in all instinctive self-expressions real sacraments abound. Outward and visible signs with inward and spiritual grace are everywhere. They are mystic, not magic. Let's do our own sacraments!

Sacraments on every hand? Would any lover be satisfied with the dictionary definition of a kiss as a "release of a slight vacuum in the buccal cavity of the face, in contact with the surface of another's integument, resulting in a slightly sibilant sound as the lips part?" Ask the wife or mother welcoming a lad back from Korea if there is not a sacramental validity in her kiss. Sacraments are even in the less dramatic field too. A gentlemen doffs his hat to a lady. The courtesy is more than the physical gesture. It carries a gentility which graces the social relations of man and woman above animality. We shake hands, not as in the olden days, because that act prevented the sword hand from flying to the sword hilt, but because we grasp a friend by it. These are sacraments, great and small.

Each sacrament has three aspects. There is something done bodily, something understood mentally, and something known in the spirit. Here, for instance, is a letter from my mother. It is rag paper covered with ink marks. It has a faint fragrance from the lavender in her drawer. I hold the letter in my hand and look at it; I catch the whiff of lavender. That is what I do with my body. My mind interprets the ink marks on the paper. It makes sense of the words. I understand what she has written; mind meets mind. Yet as I read there is more than the grammatical sense of the words. They have the flavor of her personality. They are characteristic. *She* grows *present,* spirit to spirit. Her presence is not a *thereness* inside the envelope or confined to the grammar of her sentences. The letter is sacramental. Long after she is dead, it will bring *her* to me. It will convey a real presence.

So it is with all symbols which convey vital gifts. Sacraments are as simple as that. They are holy with life. Human nature rises to them because they are vehicles of that divinity that shapes our ends.

If we cannot cleanse and lift the two most typical sacraments of the Church until they enlist our heartfelt naturalness; if churchianity has spoiled them beyond rescue of their essence; we may have to turn from the blasphemy of their magic pretense and the more elevate our informal, uncopyrighted, lay sacraments until our everyday simplicities and spontaneities are transfigured by our hallowing of them.

THE CONGREGATION

Thus far we have talked of the individual and his worship. There is one more note to be struck, the note of *togetherness* in all this. For a church building is where a congregation assembles. And a congregation differs from an audience. The members of an audience remain more insulated from each other than the members of a congregation ever do. It is this audience attitude which kills worship. Something more than side by side adjacency is in a true congregation.

We belong together. We find in comradeship a strength which lone existence cannot equal. Ask the truly married man or woman whether life is richer now that it is a mutuality than it was while single. Ask the sincere Mason why he belongs to that fellowship. Ask the baseball fan why he roots for the home team. Ask the orchestra member why he loves to play in the Symphony. For that matter, why does the Symphony audience come to Symphony Hall for a concert? There are radios and television sets which would allow each attendant to stay at home in his living room to hear and see. The answer is that at home there is no such shared experience as the Symphony audience knows. It is actually a congregation. Its unity under the spell of magnificent music is a worship. Its applause is its antiphon; its possession by music is a mystical adventure. The notes on the orchestra scores, the horsehair and catgut of the violins, the oddly shaped oboes, clarinets, kettle drums, and the brasses are media, outward and audible. They are all for music, the music which seized deaf Beethoven, blind Bach, or Brahms for its voicing, so to sway the emotions of this future congregation by that which the mind cannot define but to which the soul surrenders.

Worship should be based on enough kinship of spirit — not identity of opinion — to weld all into a membership one of another in the aspirations and inspirations which are beyond all words. Religion is not belief but a living force, first of all; afterward there can be examination of the dower it brings. Worship first catches the inexpressible surge of reality, "high and lifted up." Then the appraisal can come.

This may sound utopian, too ideal. But shall we lower the ideal to the actual or strive to lift the actual toward the ideal? If the idealist can hold his ideal fast there will be ways to pry open tight-shut windows in consecrated churches in which humorless piety has grown stuffy, and where mellifluous shamanism has sucked the oxygen out of the air. There is a chance sent by crisis to begin making over the churches into fresh power. Liberalism is already at work. The future is with it; its ideal is at work with leavening power. If those who feel the pressure for freer worship would rise up and join in the cry for liberation, there might be victory past our dreaming — together.

CHAPTER THIRTEEN

What Has Science To Say?

In every department of his thinking the usual modern is roughly scientific, *except in religion.* He may not guess how fully his practical life has been permeated by the general ideology of science, nor how far removed he is from the pre-scientific attitude — except in religion. Millions of moderns lean toward the scientific approach although they have no slightest expertness in the experimental or deductive techniques of professional scientists. The author of this book is among science's very lay folk. He makes no pretensions to laboratory qualifications or to the understanding of relativity's curved space. But he and all of us should do some brain-stretching along factual lines and push ourselves out into wider inquiry about universals.

Certainly most of us wall ourselves mentally into the narrow cell of our immediate concerns, with murky, small windows giving only the vaguest outlook. Religion's sunlight is dimmed by our incuriosity, and our view of reality is scaled down to the near-by and the tangible.

It is the presupposition of all mental endeavor, animating all our detective-story research and deductive science, that *reality is intelligible.* That is, *our minds are fitted to understand reality because our minds and reality are related by their nature.* Our minds are a part of reality. They are consanguine. In turn, it follows that *our minds and the Infinite are akin in their activity.* As Yum Yum says in *The Mikado,* "Nature is lovely and rejoices in her loveliness; I am a child of Nature and I take after my mother." So with deeper awe and sincerer humility we proudly say that we are the children of the life force and take after its nature — that is, if we live true to our potentialities.

Deductions may therefore be entirely logical. They can assume that the universe is consistent; that reality, including creativity itself, abides faithful; that natural law is knit into the laws of psychation; and that what occurs on this grain of stardust is the local manifestation of the universal enterprise. We can argue from the small to the great, from the human to the Infinite.

May we borrow from a moving and great book, insufficiently known, *Behind the Universe,* by the late Louis Berman, M.D.? [1] He evidently had steeped himself in Bergson's epochal and directive book, *Creative Evolution,* but carries his argument beyond it. He writes:

In the ancient mythology of the Scandinavians there was a tree, the Tree of the World, Yggsdrasil. It was an ash tree, the roots and branches of which reached everywhere, binding together the earth, heaven and hell. That tree is the perfect symbol and image of the range and span of individual and collective conscious and unconscious, and the all-inclusive psychic circulation, at the heart of which is all that which may be called the superconscious. In the totality of the tree's structure the individual may be a leaf or a bud, rootlet, seed or fruit. Bonds visible and invisible weave all of individuality's life along every direction of time and space into the substances and energies of every other life which has been, is, or will be, within the psychic collectivity which unites them into a single being. . . . The essence of the cosmic process is psychic in nature and structure, and that life and that process are integrated in a single cosmic plan and movement.

He therefore speaks of "psychation," which is a good, useful word.

---

[1] Louis L. Berman, *Behind the Universe: A Doctor's Religion* (New York, 1943).

The churches have not stretched the minds of the faithful to any such ideas. It is both amusing and ghastly that with all the nominal talk of the God whom the heaven of heavens cannot contain, they still give the impression that this tiny world and its human history are God's sole or favored interest and that a cross on the barren hill outside Jerusalem's walls is his central and magic-making focus in the whole universe. Copernicus proved that our earth is not the hub of creation but a peripheral minor satellite of the sun. Up to his day the Ptolemaic idea was taken as final, which egotistically placed our molecule as the pivot of all significance. Genesis and the rest of the Old Testament cosmology took for granted that, as in Joseph's bumptious dream, the sun and moon and the eleven stars made obeisance to humanity. So Copernicus was damned and Galileo was forced to renounce his expanded conviction, and the Church still parries their findings. More obstinately, it evades the implications of modern astronomy's telescope revelations of galaxies, whirling nebulae, the drift of the universe of universes, and of the stages of stellar evolution in the infinite whole.

The pageantry of this frightens weaklings into evasion of its consequences for world-centered religion. The Church continues to dodge even Copernican findings, to say nothing of Mt. Wilson and Mt. Palomar science. The hypothesis of cosmic evolution either is attacked by bibliolaters as impious or is put in the department of irrelevant information. Our working thesis is centered on this tiny globe with its anthill politics and its moilings for food, sex, and conquest.

Does astronomy annihilate creedal faith? If the nebula of Andromeda, the most distant constellation or universe visible to the naked eye, is nine hundred thousand light years away, and if our sun is merely an insignificant one among thousands of millions of other suns (as it is), how is it possible for us to stand up and say, "I believe in God the Father, maker of Heaven and Earth" with any Ptolemaic idea still as the setting of that creed? [2]

To admit, for instance, that Mars may be inhabited, forces a humility which we defensively oppose. Yet it is unjustifiably snobbish to assume that nowhere in the unencompassed totality, at any moment in its aeonic history, has there been the equivalent of our humanity with its mental and emotional evolution. Doctrinally, it is insolent to parade the Prophet of Nazareth as God's *only* Son in all the universe. Poor Mars, for instance, if there were no such hero and incarnation there! Just as it is unimaginable that anywhere in the cosmos two plus two do not make four or that values are not values, so it is unthinkable that the "psychergia" (to use another of Dr. Berman's pet words) of God should not build up its consequences in fulfillments wherever, whenever, and however it is realized. We hesitate to speak in the old terminology of a personal God, because the ascription of personality is so weak and so loaded with limiting connotations of the old Genesis pattern that we have an immediate mental picture of a white-haired Super-Jupiter on a throne just above

[2]And now, according to the announcement from Mt. Wilson and Mt. Palomar observatories, we must revise our former ideas of the size of the universe. Instead of the universe being two billion years old, it is upward of four billion. And instead of the farthest reaches of space being a billion light years, it seems more likely that our estimate must now penetrate twice that far. Such a linear doubling of dimensions, when multiplied three times to get the volume, would represent an eightfold increase in the size of the universe. Two "new" populations of stars have been found, also, the first characterized by "blue light" stars of very high temperatures, one hundred thousand times as bright as the sun; and the second consisting predominantly of "red light" stars of much lower temperature, only one thousand times as bright as the sun. The stars hitherto used as yardsticks in computing the dimensions of the universe have been discovered as belonging to different groups, not to the same one; therefore the new measuring standard. Our little earth is seen still more as a molecule in the suburbs of space.

the bowl of the firmament. Yet all we know of personality must have its source in a God of the universe whose more-than-human dynamic is the creative power within all Creation. Therefore it has come to pass that a thinking person must now hesitate before he uses the name "God" at all.

The name "God" is an empty container to be filled with whatever concepts we individually have. There is no word easier to use without deep meaning. How few actually conceive of God as in Spinoza's hypothesis, "contemporaneous with all time, coextensive with all space and all existence everywhere and forever, embracing all transmutations and all realized potentialities of existence through all eternity."

If, to repeat Gerald Heard's phrase, "faith is the resolve to give the highest possible meaning to all we know," then we are indeed in for a revamping and aeration of our petty, vestigial concepts. "Le lieu défini est le dieu fini," particularly if the definition is not up to the indications of science plus the humanities. Those of us who at all hold to the Gestalt psychology will feel its compulsion to extend our thinking into a pattern which indicates a greater God whose being is itself a continual becoming, leavening the whole with its urge to complete the unity. We human beings are not the sole advolutionists, who are forever tormented with the divine discontent of *Prägnanz,* i.e., the inner discomfort inherent in a felt incompleteness, compelling effort to achieve our part in the whole's fulfillment. The *"psychergia"* of all creative, universally developmental, salvaging, spiritualizing, pervasive, qualitative, mutualizing, refining life is in that whole, making it more than the sum of its parts.

Science deals with such facts as our status on this little earth exposes to its scrutiny, analysis, and deduction. But science deals with only one aspect of reality; the soul is outside its orbit. Bertrand Russell flatly puts science in its proper place, saying, "Questions as to 'values' — that is to say, as to what is good or bad on its own account, independently of its effects — lie outside the domain of science." And again, "Science must not obtrude upon the sphere of values, and scientific technique . . . must not outweigh the ends which it should serve." [3] But personality in its turn cannot disregard its relationship to science as also legitimately a part of the Gestalt; the scientific *method* should also rule in the field of self-comprehension and its implications. "God" is the magnetic pole of both compasses. The magnetic field of reality is the total area in which "God" is experienced.

Is all of this too abstruse? A homelier analogy is feasible: *"God is to his universe as I am to my body."* This gives a workable and satisfying clue, from small to great, from our own inside information to total inference.

(1) Infinite space does not contradict this analogy. The proportion of space is the same in the molecule and in the empyrean. Light years may separate Orion from the Pleiades or Betelgeuse, but light years are in much the same ratio of distance as between the elements in an atom, where we are told the components are as far from each other as single tennis balls per five-acre lot. If one's body is an organic whole, so the body of God can be.

(2) The human body is made of cells. Each cell lives a life of its own, with specialized function but in symphonic orchestration with all the others grouped in bones, muscles, nerves, blood corpuscles, hormones, and brain. There are gradations of function, too, according to the degree of psychation in the total brain, with more sensitiveness to life than

[3]*Religion and Science*, p. 242; *The Scientific Outlook*, p. 266.

bone and cartilage possess. The spirit of the individual uses the brain and nerve system for its directive thought and will. The unity of body, mind, and spirit makes the person.

Each of us is a cell in the body of God, according to our capacity. The psychation in human beings is certainly more vital than in inert matter (although we know now that matter is not material, since its atomic structure is of active force). In all gradations of universal existence matter is transcended by life, and life shades up into humanity's mind and will and incarnates itself in individualities. This would properly be the fact also in other long-evolving worlds, where some attainment greater than we have glimpsed here may surpass our amateur qualities. Yet there is organic coherence in the body's correlation, except when there is defiance of it in some spot.

(3) Evil is malignant disease in the body of God. Sin is the refusal to correlate oneself in its organic life. It is the individualistic denial of life's greater potentialities. It is reversion to one-celled selfishness in opposition to the thrust of evolution. It attempts civil war in the body. It affronts the divine. It spawns enmity. Yet, if there were no next step for organic life, selfish individualism might be normal. Every one of the seven deadly sins would be justified on the lower level of competition. Gluttony, sloth, lust, hate, envy, slander, and thieving are all natural to tooth and claw survivals. If there were no realization of the inner command toward organic unity even war would be justified for selfish power.

(4) When there is disease or pain in one's body, the forces of his life combine to overcome the rebellion and exorcise the evil. Healing begins by the powers of the physical and the spirit. Unless the evil is too virulent it is barricaded or

conquered. In the body of God there are major rebellions, too. Racial antagonisms, class conflicts, all secular and ecclesiastical bigotry, unilateral aggressions of all kinds, malice, exploitations and prideful materialism are our earth's malignant virus working against the health and "wholth" of God's being. And who knows what forces conspire with those we ourselves set to work? It is surely an affair of moment for the universe and its spirit.

(5) Persons are God's agents. The Greek and Roman theaters had quaint conventions. Actors wore great masks representing the comic or tragic protagonists of the play. From the lips of the actor to the opening of the masks, wide mouths, small megaphones were fitted. The masks were likewise meant to subordinate the actor to his role, which was greater than he. The Latins called these masks *personae,* "through which the voice comes forth." From this derivation comes "person": the outer individual through which comes the utterance of personality. Then the thought went deeper until the inner self was thought of as the *persona* of a super-person. Therefore in a better than Trinitarian mood we can say that there are an infinite number of persons and but one God.

(6) Man's chronic unhappiness has been due to the poisonous privacies and destructive discontents of his too insulated individuation. He has been engaged continually in a search for the wider meanings of his individuality and in the quest for a way and a formula of release from the chains of self. "Now he has become aware that his innermost suffering, keenest of all pains, is due to his withdrawal from the total life-personality and the contraction into himself of the vast possibilities of the psychic life. Man's search for significance in his existence and a road to contentment can be satisfied

only in the achievement of a progressive harmony between his consciousness and the whole of life." [4] Or in Robert Browning's lines:

> To give me once again the electric snap and spark
> Which prove, when finger finds out finger in the dark
> O' the world, there's fire and life there, link but hands
> And pass the secret on. Lo, link by link, expands
> The circle, lengthens out the chain, till one embrace
> Of high with low is found uniting the whole race. . . .
>
> Clash forth life's common chord, whence, list how they ascend
> Harmonies far and faint, till our perception end—
> Reverberated notes whence we construct the scale
> Embracing what we know and feel and are![5]

[4] Louis Berman again; paralleling Henri Bergson, *Creative Evolution*, Chapter I.
[5] "Fifine at the Fair," XCI and LXII.

CHAPTER FOURTEEN

Is Immortality Logical?

Bruce Bairnsfather's Old Bill, crouched in his shell hole beside his buddy, ruminates to his comrade, "Ain't we infinities?" Dug into the battlefield of our physical existence here, under the barrage of its exploding problems, pains, joys, and mysteries, do we feel with Old Bill? Are we infinities? Are we immortal?

Perhaps it makes little day-by-day difference to decent men and women whether immortality can be proved. They are doing their best at the job of living. What will be, will be, they say. Our speculations and deductions will not decide whether there is immortality ahead or what its nature will be if there is. And we are so sense-bound by the conditions of the flesh and its data that we would be unable to know with any scientific accuracy what are the conditions of a life, if any, outside our present range, and greater than our maximum analysis.

Nevertheless, there would be a ratification of our struggle for worths if we could gain a reasonable assurance that they have some lasting authority. Most of all, it would be of real comfort to feel that character and its uniqueness may not be dissipated but that the obvious incompleteness of personality here and now may have a more spacious and rich development beyond. For we all instinctively feel that there are possibilities for us for which we have no full chance now, try as we will.

Homer may have complained pessimistically that life ought not to be like the sand castles a child painstakingly constructs on the seashore which the next tide will dissolve. The analogy has often been suggested, too, of Michelangelo's snow image when there was a snowfall in Florence and the arbitrary pope commanded him to carve a snow statue. We can imagine the mood of that volcanic genius as he put his skill into an image which would melt in the next morning's sun. So with carving out a personality. We want some faith that it is of enduring worth.

Gone for all but the literalists are the ideas of any Dante-esque hell, purgatory, paradise, and heaven, compartmentalized and definite. Yet the Church's official concepts have not been disentangled from those Dark Age impossibilities. The Church still officially speaks of a divisional afterlife and of eternal reward and punishment in its definite zones. The Last Judgment is still the bogie to scare the credulous out of sin. Revivalists can still threaten hell fire, and the Roman Church can still draw its maps of the celestial and infernal realms. And bewildered, loving amateurs at faith grope on in a fog of disquiet, trying to believe what is repudiated by their own best instincts — instincts which are better than the medieval or primitive God who is not yet doctrinally discarded.

What minister has not been deeply touched by the anguish of mourning people whose dear ones are said by the Church and the mortician to have "passed" over "the great gulf fixed" into the "Beautiful Isle of Somewhere"? The earth has been sprinkled on the coffin, the officiant has read some liturgic benediction which says, "Earth to earth, dust to dust, in sure and certain hope of the resurrection unto eternal life, through our Lord Jesus Christ, at whose coming in glorious majesty to judge the world, the earth and the sea shall give up their dead, and the corruptible bodies of those who sleep in him shall be changed and made like unto his own glorious body." 'Twixt now and that doubtful *Dies Irae,* as Hamlet says, "The rest is silence." And love will not wait until doomsday!

Spiritualism and other cultist panaceas thrive on this violation of human yearnings. Thousands of seekers for contact with those who have been their very life turn to media which the Church fails to have provided by memorial flowers on the altar, the creedal phrase of the communion of saints, and by the Easter festival so saturate with fashion. Protestantism has even forbidden prayers for the dead.

Psychic phenomena are emerging into credited status as possible data for personal survival. Although in the popular mind they are still too associated with charlatanry and Ouija board experimentation, it is foolish to deny a residuum of scientific evidence. The vagaries of trance mediumships, automatic writing, telepathy, poltergeists, and "sensitives" are unworthy of the immortals in most cases. But there must be a well-founded suspicion that, as Professor James wrote, "we must look for the science of the future very often in the dingy and mediumistic corners of the present." Even if the findings by Bligh Bond at Glastonbury were stuffily scorned (Would there were time and space to detail that dramatic tale for the Holy Grail!) and even if Sir Oliver Lodge's "Raymond" obscured his unquestionable etheric studies, to quote Sludge the Medium:

> This trade of mine—I don't know—can't be sure
> But there was something in it, tricks and all—
> All was not cheating, sir, I'm positive!

> I don't know if I move your hand sometimes
> When the spontaneous writing spreads so far.
> If my knee lifts the table all that height.
> Why the inkstand don't fall off the desk atilt,
> Why I speak so much more than I intend,
> Describe so many things I never saw,
> I tell you sir, in one sense I believe
> Nothing at all—that everybody can,
> Will, and does cheat: but in another sense
> I'm ready to believe my very self—
> That every cheat's inspired and every lie
> Quick with the germ of truth.[1]

"There's something in it," yes — but what? The general failure of psychical research evidence is the unavoidable lack of revelation as to the qualitative aspects of immortal life. Psychical research has to specialize on the demonstration of mere survival, as Dr. Hyslop once remarked, as the identity of a burglar is established by the shape of his boot heel's print in the mud. We are not content with that; incorrigibly we want to know what the immortals have learned in their new stage of life in the invisible. But, pathetically and too typically, outside a dingy spiritualist hall was the illiterately chalked announcement that Abraham Lincoln would speak there through someone's mediumship. Now Lincoln was a great man, whose utterances while on earth were noble. After almost ninety years of experience in the spiritual realm he should have something still more great to communicate and more majestically characteristic. No august word came through his "control," however; the session with his assumed spirit was devoted to bromidic triteness and trivial "messages."

---

[1]Robert Browning, "Sludge the Medium," lines 808, 809, 1311-1325.

There are more tasteful speculations sometimes, according to the cultural refinement of the agent, such as Stewart Edward White's famous *Unobstructed Universe*. But the imaginative deductions of St. John Irvine's *Sophia, Abraham's Bosom* by Basil King, Sutton Vane's play *Outward Bound,* and even Sartre's *The Chips are Down* are far more satisfying to the hungry spirit than even the scientific studies of extrasensory perception and psychical laboratory experimentation.

Eternal life is not enough. What would be its evolution into new values and truths?

Personality faces forward. It lives by values and is itself the supreme value we know. And values are developmental; they always tend to greater richness of experience. Personal living is proleptic. The classic texts — that we are saved by hope, that faith is the substance of things hoped for, the evidence of things not seen — are true with a truth that is more than scriptural. There is a magnetism from on beyond. Even at death we have barely begun to *live*.

Does our intuition of values stem from a reality which is their source? There is no effect without a cause. Are we not mere promises of what we can be, and whence comes the ideal of what we can be but from something more compelling than existence has contrived?

The small circle of light cast by a lantern is enough to show the direction of a path through the dark. A few feet ahead, a few feet either side, and a few feet behind, it travels step by step as the lantern-bearer walks forward. The circle of knowledge in our present years of existence is like this. Our little-lighted space suffices to indicate the direction life takes. We have light for the next step and we go toward the periphery of the moment's knowledge only to see it advance before us. And we know the path is headed somewhere and that the somewhere has determined its approach. Life evolves *for and by* what is to be. It is prenatal.

A baby is formed in the mother's womb for and by the life to come. In the darkness, eyes for the light of day, ears for sounds some day, lungs for the breath of life in the open air, lips and tongue for the speech which will use them, hands for grasping, feet to walk in the roads which await! The life-to-be shapes the child's embryonic recapitulation of the stages of human evolution up to our era. Evolution is *ad*volution. When at last the gestation is finished, the baby is thrust forth into the life for and by which it was formed. To the child the moment must seem like death; to the mother it is a wrenching separation from bodily unity. But this rending of the flesh is for the sake of a higher, more reciprocal unity of mind and spirit, that the child may be a person among persons. The future has claimed it.

The child grows. Adulthood exercises its sway on that growth. What will be makes the progressive changes from infancy to childhood to youth, to manhood or womanhood. When adult physique has been attained, the demand of growth stops, surely with the implication that the prenatal personality has now reached the stature which will utilize this machinery for its adult will. Within the advolutionary bodily life, as in another womb, what we call *psychation* has been beginning. Character is incubating. It is not yet fully formed, perhaps. Yet whatever its perfection, it is always at a beginning, a birth. Let any callow youngster say he is in love! He is, but what that love will be when deepened, mellowed, tested by pains and mutualities through the years until marriage is transfigured into its ineffable sanctities of oneness! Work to do, aspirations to fulfill, wisdom to acquire and use, influence to exert, selfhood to give — it all lies ahead, and the ideal builds the actual. Stirring like the unborn child, straining against uterine enclosure by the five senses, the self obeys the future.

For we feel the limitations of our present circumstances. They so obstinately inhibit the completer liberty we wish for. If I could *only* be understood by you from within your mind! But I am dependent on air waves, ear drums, nerve vibrations, and your interpretation of them; or through the printed page I am handicapped by the trickiness of semantic words, until I almost despair of making my full meaning *felt*. So each one of us protests. We are attempting to overcome separateness in every way. Communications bring us closer. Membership in this or that organization, party, Masonry, church, clique, chorus, club, or family is a defiance of insulation. Love is the supreme declaration of independence against separateness, the most effective struggle to transcend isolation.

Faith and hope are temporary virtues, interim intuitions. Faith is not yet clear sight and apprehension. Its clues lead out past present vision. Hope is an embryonic sensibility of the soul which someday will function as something better than a hunch. It is not a hazarded hypothesis without guidance, but it is not a validating consummation; it is for the moment the defiance of all that contravenes its climax. Hope is not truly hope until things seem hopeless. Then it attains the beauty and strength of the proleptic. It says,

> Oh, self beyond self I call my soul,
> Climb up into the crow's nest!
> Look out over the tumbling waters;
> Warn me of reefs and storm!

No, there is no substitute for you—
Up into the crow's nest, O my soul!

Therefore it is prefigured that by the event we on this side of it call death but which from the yon side apparently is another birth, the prenatally developed personality enters the kind of life for and by which it has been shaped. Immortality is retroactive. It builds immortability.

Immortability? Unkillableness, such vital selfhood that "it cannot be holden of death." There is a doctrine held by some that immortality, while sure for the strong self, is none too certain for the self so weak in qualitative realities that it would be stillborn and perish. If a self is not compounded of immortabilities, how can it survive? If immortality has not been gestated during physical life, how can it have its continuance? The thought is sobering. It sounds logical. But the process of creativity by that which is to be is still the intention of life, is it not?

Immortality would be the unhampered opportunity for all the powers with which the pregnancy stage has been at work. That Gestaltist principle of the *Prägnanz* which leavens all our labor for wholeness of patterning has application in this. Delivered from the flesh, flesh conditions will not intervene in person-to-person indwellings. Geography will not get in the way and keep lives apart. Time will not regulate souls by the clock. The reign of the brain's gray matter and of the five senses will be over. Communications will be by-passed. The person will be the direct experience of others. The heaven ahead will be the indwelt heaven of souls.

If a radium spark is examined under a fluoroscope, it's said, it will be seen sending out a veritable shower of sparks, each as large and as bright as the parent spark. Yet the parent spark does not diminish. Whether or not this is up-to-date science, it is a good, though weak, analogy for the immortal personality, here and now or more freely, later. Self-contributions are of many varieties; they should be more untrammeled forthgivings after death. The mystical instincts we now feel gestating in our natures are the creative motivations from the selves we may be in our ex-carnation to come.

It is a very subsidiary and comparatively unimportant query — purely a scientific curiosity of the sense mind — whether there will be some organic vehicle by means of which personality will act. Let's try a few deductions.

This new-born organic vehicle for self cannot be a here-or-there organism bound by locale or matter. That's clear.

This present body of flesh draws its material from the resources of its earthly habitat. But each particle of the earth which is incorporated is very temporarily of its substance. (We may leave aside the puzzling new concepts of physics which affirm that matter is only force, for at any rate whatever matter is it is not spirit, and it acts with earthy substantiality.) The skin of the palm of a hand is changed every fourteen days, and is renewed. The enamel of the teeth is changed every fourteen years and is renewed. Averaging so, every five years, the body has returned its dust to the dust. *What does the replacing?* The fingertip of a fifty-year-old man has been replaced six hundred thousand times, yet every minute whorl and loop of his fingerprint is identical since birth. What made the dust of it fall into that exact pattern? The same question is to be asked of all the other forms of the organism.

The only rational conclusion must be that there is some

invisible, controlling, permanent, etheric, organic entity, a living and animating "spiritual body" which is immune to the deaths of the flesh with an aliveness not touched by dissolution.

This etheric body — to quote Paul with modern synonyms for what he calls "a body for spirit" — is the tool of the self which is its sovereign. Dust has no sensation except as it is infused with this etheric body's sensitivity. When this etheric body drops dust, dust returns to disintegrated dusthood. At death it would seem logical that the momentary ninety cents' worth of chemicals which comprise the dust just then would be shed or released to the elements. That is death. That is all there is to it; the etheric body is no longer loaded with the dust it used in the former chapter. The living self is freed from encumbrance, but an etheric body would be no encumbrance. Rather would it be a tool of freer activity.

This is only a guess, but isn't it a likely one? It would certainly chime in with many psychical phenomena under perceptive conditions. And it would accord with the yearning of heart-rent mourners who cry out, "Shall we recognize one another?" Why not? The familiar lineaments will be perceived, not merely seen. Sight will be bettered by insight. The unique person will be unmistakable. We may well hope for a sublimation and transfiguration of our present human relationships. Why shouldn't I know my own? My embrace should be more than arms can compass. The spiritual body would be the means of my soul's hold on my beloved. Why not?

Taken only from the laboratory point of view and analyzed without pious indoctrination, the resurrection attributed to Jesus was evidently more than a simple immortality of memory or influence. It has to be tied into the category of mystic or psychic report such as seems to come from exceptional attunement and openness with even unexpectant subconscious kindred. Good Friday was a ghastly test to any further belief in Jesus by his friends. They could not disbelieve in what he had been to their hearts and minds, but he was evidently just too good to be true. A callous and brutal world had spurned the rightness of this life. In panic, mad and horrible, they fled. But *something* happened, a something which transformed them to conquering proclaimers that the death of their Master had been only a death of his body. He was alive — vibrantly, definitely, personally set free from the carpenter's flesh. The original record of this may be overlaid by the smothering superstition of a resuscitated corpse and an empty tomb, but that original testimony plainly indicates something quite other than so magically crude a miracle. It shows a mystical vindication of Jesus' personal being, in which the recognizability of an etheric body is incidental to the comfort of his closeness to their own being. A supreme person would naturally be felt with more qualitative intensity than any person of less vital reality.

What of visions, then? An objective appearance is relayed to the brain by light rays and eye reactions, but the ultimate *awareness,* so to speak, is at the inner end of the optic nerve where the mysterious conversion of stimulus into consciousness takes place. The stimuli of sound and contact are converted into hearing and touch sense in the brain. That is a commonplace, although a mystery no one has fathomed. If there should be a presence which takes strong hold of a percipient, his awareness of that presence would be person-to-person — that is, it would register on the consciousness of its affinity, *within* his life. Thought activity would then be

keyed up by the awareness so much that it might well stir
the habitual nerves of the five senses at their inner terminus,
until the consciousness falls into the pattern of sight and
touch and hearing, when the objectivity of the presence is
not necessarily outside the body at all. The fact is that the
presence is in the mind and heart of the mystic, merged into
his essential, central self and taking possession of his lesser
senses at the same moment.

Visions are not alien to our human nature and its adventures. If they come, they ought to be judged according to
the evidence of their conveyed worth to the spirit, lest bad
dreams or hallucinations of subconscious vaporings should
delude us. If they come — oh so exceptionally — they are
not to be sensationalized as though they are of eerie significance. They are by-products, under understandable conditions, of a strong awareness of a presence. The normal thing
would be more quiet, the spirit-to-spirit self-contribution at
the *roots* of our being, life into life, known by its results in
new peace, new insight, the new leavening of what we are.

If God (by any definition of him) is so often anonymous
in his permeation of life, losing himself to find himself in
us for the help he can be in us to be ourselves, so would our
personal saints be to us.

Immortality is not automatic. It is not eternity. Thoreau
was mistaken when on his deathbed he admonished a friend,
"One world at a time; one world at a time." That isn't possible. Life is one sweeping advolution, an *élan vital*. Granted
that it has its possibilities of thwarted growth, admitted that
there are perverse folk who flout or fixate or reverse the
process back toward animality, nevertheless the possibility
of the next stage is evident. A fiery exhorter once ranted to

his congregation, "Oh brethren, if any word of mine has kindled a new spark of the spirit in you, Oh brethren, water that spark!" But unconsciously, perhaps, as we go about our daily work and play and humanities, most of us are not watering the spark of immortality but nursing it to a steady flame. Our dreams, our best decencies, our loves and righteous indignations, our characteristic trends of selfhood — all are beginnings of what must be. The text, "In my father's house are many mansions" actually says in the original, "In my father's realm are many caravanseries." Caravanseries are inns on the road, inns where there can be rest after a day's journey, refreshment, invigoration for the next day's travel on beyond. The road is a never-finished "becoming"; it is the road of immortality.

If our best deductions and our highest instincts are not fulfilled exactly as we have fallibly reasoned, we may rest assured that the immortal reality, according to all indications of the spirit, will be better, not worse, than their prophecy. We cannot think greater thoughts or hope for better blessings than reality has in store. We are not greater than the divine. When and if, newborn by death, we begin the adventure of life still more abundant, our first realization will be "Why, of course!"

CHAPTER FIFTEEN

Comrades of the Carpenter!

The frontispiece of a boyhood book pictured the plowing of Achilles. In it Achilles holds the plow handles. His cerulean cloak billows out behind him, against the daffodil-yellow sunrise. His three superb horses haul the plowshare through the crusted earth—Xanthos, Balios, and the goodly Pedasos.

Xanthos and Balios were miraculous steeds, sired by the West Wind, of one of the winged Harpies, endowed with speech. Their silver hooves scarcely dented the soil. Their beauty and strength was beyond earthly glamor.

But their yokemate was otherwise. The goodly Pedasos was everything that his name — the Plodder — implied. He was a heavy-haunched, iron-necked, sturdy farm horse, whose patient readiness made him an apt trace horse between the prancing miracle-pair. He kept them down to their labor; he provided the necessary balance for their temperamental splendor. They needed him and he needed them.

Here's a ready-made simile, from which a lesson has been self-evident since classic Greece. Let Xanthos stand for our ideals and Balios for our understanding; Xanthos of the spirit, Balios of the mind. They are born of some mystic parentage; they have majesty and beauty and truth. But Pedasos is grim grit and unflinching realism. Without him the supernal two are only impulses and visions. With him, the three get heavy plowing done.

Weaklings, sentimentalists, and pietists hate the slow labor of applied conviction. Unfortunately, however, there is no magic which brings results; they must be earned by hard labor. Labor is the word for work and for birth pains. So is travail. Character is dependent on ideals and understanding, of course, but it must have dogged determination as well, a will sufficient for drudging resoluteness against inertia and opposition. Religion is as religion does, by commitment to practice.

At its most, the definition of religion is the yoking of Xanthos emotion and Balios understanding. At its least, it is Xanthos without Balios. Although the Church's sacraments and sermons are specified for inspiration for better living, the fact is that this incentive may be used by self-serving "personal religion" individualists. Comforted and strengthened individuals may, and perhaps do, go into their natural relationships with a more mellow or charitable personal intention. Even by pious sentimentalism in their church life they may perhaps be helped to personal peace or sweeter character. The Ten Commandments and the stipulations of churchly regularism may curry individual members into semi-blamelessness. Yet on the whole is it unfair to say that traditional churchmanship loves cushioned pews more than it loves cleaning Augean stables, Hercules fashion? In its corporate capacity, is the Church more devoted to inside concerns than it is to working toward the solution of major social problems? Applied Christianity would harness Pedasos into the traces with Xanthos and Balios for organized practicality's attack on encrusted conditions. But has the organized Church such realism? That is the question.

To be sure, humanitarian projects abound. And it is utterly true that they have been set up and run by dynamic individuals *on their own*. They have been stirred by their own innate compulsions and some instinctive vision of the Son of Man, who has not been quite obliterated for them by ecclesiastical screening. As individuals, but not as accredited agents of the organized Church, they have changed out of their Sunday clothes, rolled up their sleeves, and challenged social inequities with bare hands. Their seven-day-a-week social service is both religiously motivated and sturdily constructive; but, be it repeated, their Pedasonian enthusiasm is to their own *individual* credit. They combine in humanitarian movements of far-seeing compassion and high resolve; they live their actual faith into its successes from sheer joy of helping human beings out of quicksands onto solid ground. They ask no halo for what they do. They would be embarrassed to admit that their motives are religious. They have no knowledge how Christly their busy saviorhood is. They happen spontaneously to be drawn into alleviative activities because they have hearts for others in hard luck or weakness; but they are too occupied with their tasks in hand to realize the high Christian-ness of Red Cross, Community Fund, Hospital Board, Alcoholics Anonymous, Child Placement, Rehabilitation Center, or "Y."

The social conscience is sensitized. It has been alerted to awareness of long-smothered injustices and maladjustments. Under the prodding of an awakened sense of responsibility to right wrongs, our society squares around to its job. Through government, through private charities, through community surveys and engineerings, *but not through the divided churches in any efficient social physicianship,* the body corporate of society at large is at work on its ills.

The multitudinousness of the problems now on the soul of the constructive minority to such an extent that something is done about them is indeed staggering. But the knowledge of this multitudinousness is not discouraging in itself. If problems exist, it is better to have them uncovered where we can see them for what they are. Every sensitization of the social conscience is progress, although it begins with a pain in the mind. The Golden Rule has forced itself into wider and wider application — until it has become far more than a copybook maxim. Pain is the incentive to cure what is advertised by it as wrong; therefore it is all to the good if comrades are stirred by their pain in the mind or soul to get busy. Racial intolerance, economic injustices (working both ways), *really* un-American activities of all kinds, cheap political bunkum, power politics great and small, bigotry, the conspiracy against the wholesomeness of youth, erotic intensifications, sectionalism, name-calling, slums, under-housing, manipulated inflation or depression, prison and insane asylum barbarities, the seepage of ideals out of utilitarian education, fascist or Communist ideology in open or disguised forms, witch-hunting, the spread of psychoneuroses, the fever of gadget-possession — the list of problems seems endless!

But realists stake out long-range objectives and take immediate steps.

The eleventh chapter of Hebrews could therefore be paraphrased with contemporary mentions of a faith which gives substance to ideals, somewhat as follows: "What shall I more say? For the time would fail me to tell of the United Nations' endeavors, of public health agencies, of slum clearances, of old-age aid and workmen's compensation, and of the uses of psychiatry for the mentally ill, of the revolution in farming methods by the machine, and of the new bacteriology and clinical medicine and health insurance, and of the new educational programs; which, through the Golden Rule, subdued petty nationalisms, worked out the righting of manifold wrongs, obtained promises of social justice, stopped the mouths of demagogues, quenched the violence of fanatics, escaped the edge of antipathy's sword, out of weakness made men and women stronger, waxed valiant in the fight for human rights, turned to flight armies of aliens to the common good."

The melting pot of our era was volcanically stirred to its veriest depths by the war. Our peacetime (*sic!*) proves it was not merely thinly skimmed of roily froth. All the problems which have been hinted at are components of one fundamental one which now looms with frightful ominousness, surpassing the threat of the H-bomb. It is the problem of a thoroughgoing social justice more drastic than we have ever before attempted.

On a new, stringent, uncompromising scale, chastising an effete civilization with its scorpions, humaneness rises up to assert its inalienable duty. *Here is a real day of judgment.* The challenge is the old one: "What shall it profit a man to gain the whole world and lose his own soul? What shall a man give in exchange for his soul?"

The history of the world has been a succession of dooms vented on civilizations which had settled on their lees of tools and possessions and vaunted achievements. Each such thing-minded civilization, preening itself in wrong pride, was invaded by simple, tough realists who took over without airs and graces. It was never a balm-and-honey time while revolutions were happening. Least of all is it one now. But the Golden Rule is unleashed. The flaming giant of humaneness (once named Jesus, perhaps) has his scourge of small cords in his hand and is routing vested selfishnesses at least from a place of *worship,* to make it a house of reality for *all.*

But social service movements are dangerously dissociated from organized religion. Organized religion has failed to relate itself in any vital way with organized labor for the betterment of human existence. The nominal deference which social service has paid to the Church by having some parson say a half-noticed grace at a kick-off dinner or by including some Church official *ex officio* on a board, for prestige, is inorganic. The Church may set up its own charities for its own obvious charges, but these are not really integrated into society's less limited schemes. *The churches remain peripheral to the main movements of social compassion.* The parable of the Good Samaritan has disconcerting relevance for priest-and-Levite churchianity then or now.

The Church is unincluded as a potent factor in wide social movements. That is the sad, predominant opinion among average people. The Church just isn't counted on to exert powerful constructive influence on world conditions or society in the large. How can it, under the incubus of its divisions? And, to state the Church's own estimate of its function, it isn't the business of the Church, *as such,* to take hold of society's practical troubles; the Church's business is with its own membership, to pluck brands from the burning, to provide personalized blessings and mystical assurance, to preach "the simple Gospel," and to trust its members to express themselves as they see fit in their individual roles as labeled Christians!

It has been sarcastically epigrammed that the gospel was a resolution referred to a committee which has gone into executive session, out of which it will not be reported for action. Or, that the common stock of the gospel has been so watered by the directors that it is almost valueless on the open market, the directors having kept the preferred stock for themselves.

Although this book may have seemed bitter against ecclesiasticism as a perversion of real religion, its arraignment actually has been reluctant. We are dissecting a tragedy. We are dealing with human lives in a crisis of history. Does the Church hear the command for analytic objectivity about itself? Do we hear the repetition of the Son of Man's agonized cry against hardened institutionalism: "O Jerusalem, Jerusalem, thou that killest the prophets and stonest those who are sent unto thee, how often would I have gathered thy children together, even as a hen gathereth her chickens under her wings, and ye would not. Behold, your house is left unto you desolate." Do we hear the reverberation of this, or is there the possibility of forestalling it by a new re-formation?

Is a new re-formation possible, forced by the cross-fertilization of realism and truly christian faith — a re-formation for the good both of the church, and of society, which is the more important?

Secularism needs a spiritual dynamic. Without it, it runs out of human sensitivity and personal compassion. No one can invent a perpetual motion machine, either mechanical or social, which will run by its own momentum. Already, inside society's agencies of social service, we can see the beginnings of bureaucratic impersonalism. People become cases, generalizations override exceptions, government takes over and tends to socialize and legally provide classified

groups with blanket remedies for common denominator age
or economic conditions. Professionalism insidiously invents
special jargons and the experts take themselves as of a superior breed as they practice their crisp efficiency techniques.
Psychiatric and out-patient coldness gets a toehold when the
case load mounts beyond the chance for conscientious individual understanding. The Church is needed in the application of humanist inspiration to the work.

It may be that the title of "church" has been so identified
with its ecclesiastical set-up that it is footless to hope that
the name could be reclaimed for what it should designate —
that inclusive, informal, working comradeship of associate
saviors which is the dream of realist christians. But perhaps
it is a waste of energy to undertake a re-education of our generation toward the better use of that name. For to the undis-
criminative vernacular people, "church" may everlastingly
imply the conventicled membership, occupied with exercises
of cultist worship and parochial programs, associated for personal benefits now and hereafter, to be had through supernatural means.

Nevertheless, inside the churches there are stirrings, mainly
incoherent, yet urgent, that the true genius of christianity
shall yet be evident. Do those who are thus stirring guess
how thorough the re-formation must be? The nuclear
minority within churchianity is not at ease in Zion; yet these
timid, cowed half-liberals, with their abstract dreams of
realism are usually far from stark decision. Shaken loose
from literalism in their inner minds, they have not fully faced
facts, the facts which would impel them to speak out.

Here and there there inside the churches are re-forming
ideas which are soon quashed. For instance, before the war
Toyohiko Kagawa is said to have ventured the theory and

experiment of a different kind of churchmanship. The startling thing about it was that it *was* startling. He would say to some humble street cleaner, perhaps, who had been converted by him, that his civic duty, carried on in the Shinkawa slum, was making living conditions there a little sweeter for home life, for the health of the children, and thus for souls' possibilities among the slum dwellers. This would be his *christian* religion in action. And his estimate of himself as a christian agent would be supplemented by his knowledge that all his christian comrades at their various posts were knit with him in an inclusive network of practical saviorhood. Applied consecration would be the natural standard of this kind of church. All its meetings for inspiration would be incentives for this essential labor. This kind of a church would be rightly known as salt of the earth. . . . But who hears much of Kagawa's idea now? It wasn't "regular."

There is something movingly magnificent in a concept of religion as a way of life. The early Christians called their church *The Way* — that is, the way of living. Faith was the inspiration, but it was not the church. An organized unity of activity under the power of the spiritual incentive was its discipleship. Is it lunacy to think forward to a modern church of such a pattern? Is it possible to hope for the development of this norm?

There will always be churches. Those churches should always be centers of inspiration and conviction. They should indeed have forms of sane worship which would be aesthetically austere but purely noble. They should have simple sacraments which would be recognizedly symbolic and interpretive of all other sacraments common to the daily life of christians. They should be served, not exploited, by non-professional ministers according to true democratic principles in the republic of God, claiming no authority not deputed to them for the common good. The cause would be the churches' discipline and joy. It would be wonderful to have an open-ended vista such as this.

Meantime, every religious realist can bring his leavening influence in churches as they are. If from within, he can help to move ecclesiasticism an inch or so out of its magic illusions, adding his voiced insurgency to the imperatives of other followers of basic ideals. If he has found sacerdotal unrealism so entrenched in separatism and dogmatism that he despairs of boring from within, he must nevertheless say what he thinks the church should be. It is not enough to shake the dust of the temple of error from off his feet and let that temple perish as he thinks it deserves. He still has the moral obligation to witness for the right. From within or from without, realists must declare their independence of the wiles of institutionalism and link hands in some fellowship of unhibited zeal for good.

Who knows whether realistic religion may not advance, here a little, there a little, constant drops of water wearing away the stone? Who knows whether some sudden, stupendous crisis of crises may not blast our world into unity on the actual fundamentals, bringing a swift, awed grasp at the true Spirit? The dire threat of the H-bomb may come true and the ride of the four horsemen of the Apocalypse through the lightnings and whirlwind of the end of our old world may be more than a nightmare dread. War with a tyrannical godlessness on a world scale (not merely with Russia) might raise up unified faith to meet its brutalities and its ideology. Our Jerusalem of familiar life, which we had thought impregnable forever, may be left with no stone on another, as we start over again in our exile from its once-presumed establishment by the Eternal. It has happened before. It can happen again. And in our hour.

Out of every previous judgment day in history, either gradual or catacylsmic, a purged new chance has always opened. Over in Babylon, with their Holy City and its Temple smashed to rubble, the prophets of the Exile firmly held that "a remnant shall return." Like the Prodigal Son, feeding swine in the far country, man may come to himself.

May it be granted that our generation can learn its lesson without a Dooms-day. The crisis is grave. More than ever it may be, however, that man's extremity is God's opportunity.

A wise father used to say to his son when that son winced at some difficulty or problem confronting him, "Son, your problems are your job. If there were no problems, there'd be no job for you. And if you've got a big problem, you've got a big job, a *great* one. Now go to it!"

Therefore our crisis is indeed *a time for greatness*. Honest realists, this is your day for it. Honest agnostics, honest philosophers simple or profound, honest theists, honest servants of the maximum truth you can glimpse, honest christians — *this is your moment*. In the interknit unity of those who faithfully will contribute their integrity and courage, *the Comrades of the Carpenter* rise up! The carpenter? A carpenter builds; he fashions shelters and dwellings for humans, where their life can be safe and serene. The hearts of his comrades respond to his *sursum corda;* they tighten their belts, square their shoulders, and cry out to the four winds:

> Now God be thanked, Who has matched us to His hour,
> And caught our youth and wakened us from sleeping,
> With hand made sure, clear eye and sharpened power.

His hour: a time for greatness of faith and of works, a time for christ-greatness of power, christ-greatness of travail for ideals, christ-greatness of religion in action. Without that christhood and what it means, the christhood operative in shared striving by realists who have shaken off compromise, where is there salvation for us?

The Comrades of the Carpenter take him off altar crosses down into their comradeship to be both their captain and the ministrant to their labor. Empty crosses anywhere in the world should signify he is not dead but living. He is down off the cross into our midst.

Realists, come out in clean-cut conviction; be ruthless with unrealism and the impertinent pretense of magic; join the Son of Man's fellowship of christhoods. How long halt ye between two opinions? Comrades of the Carpenter, your tocsin has sounded.